Great Sed

MW01010009

REVISED 4th COLOR EDITION

AN EASY-TO-USE GUIDE
FOR THE 32 GREATEST HIKING
TRAILS IN SEDONA, ARIZONA

FEATURING OUR
12 FAVORITE HIKES

William Bohan

and

David Butler

Non-liability Statement

The authors have taken every precaution to ensure that the information contained within is up-to-date, accurate and reflects trail conditions when this guide was published. However, trail conditions frequently change because of weather, Forest Service activity or other causes. The GPS data included were obtained from a Garmin model 60CSx GPS unit. Because the data are only as accurate as the sensitivity of the GPS unit, some inaccuracies may be present. Users of GPS data are urged to use common sense when hiking. Always stay on the trail. The authors, publisher, contributors, and all those involved in the preparation of this book, either directly or indirectly, disclaim any liability for injuries, accidents, and damages whatsoever that may occur to those using this guide. You are responsible for your health and safety while hiking the trails.

Acknowledgments

The authors would like to acknowledge several individuals for their contributions to this book. They are:

Our wives, Nancy Williams and Ruth Butler, for their efforts in editing this work; Wade Bell, Carole Bell, Tom Likens, Peg Likens, Jim Rostedt, Kathy Rostedt, Barrie Thomas, Grace Thomas, Darryl Thompson and Lorna Thompson for their companionship while hiking the trails.

ISBN-13: 978-1530444977

ISBN-10: 1530444977

Front Cover Photo: West Fork Trail

Table of Contents

Changes to This Edition

In this Fourth Color Edition, we added Canyon of Fools, and a totally revised Pyramid Trail. Suggestions for loop hikes are included. All individual hike maps have added detail including cumulative ascent and the trail elevation profile. Estimated hiking time as well as trail popularity have been added (see below). Trail photos, descriptions and waypoints have been updated to the latest trail conditions.

QR Code Technology

Because of space limitations, we are able to include only one representative photograph from each hike in this guide. But using mobile device technology, you can scan the QR Code found near each trail map which will give you access to additional color photos of that hike.

Cumulative Ascent Definition

The reader will notice that the maps contain "cumulative ascent" data. Elevation change simply reflects the difference between the lowest and highest elevations of the hike. Cumulative ascent reflects the ups and downs of the trail and are almost always greater than elevation change.

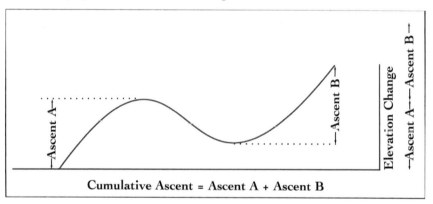

Cumulative Ascent = Ascent A + Ascent B

Hiking Time

Hiking time is estimated based on a hiking speed of between 1.5 and 2 miles per hour. Trails that have a large cumulative ascent are at the lower end of that range to allow for stops to "catch your breath." Hiking time does not include stops for snacks, photographs, meditation, etc.

Trail Popularity

The popularity of each trail is indicated by symbols (🚶🚶🚶🚶 for a very popular trail and 🚶 for a trail that isn't used very often). You should expect crowds on trails with 4 hiker symbols and likely won't encounter any other hikers on a trail that has just one hiker symbol. Weekends in Sedona tend to result in more hikers on the trails and holidays can be especially busy.

Hiking Tips

The stunning red rock formations, moderate temperatures and close proximity to the trails make hiking in Sedona an experience unlike anywhere else in the world. But hiking is not without risk. It is very important to be prepared, even for a day hike. Bring enough water to stay hydrated and drink water throughout the hike. In addition:

- Check the weather before you begin hiking and reschedule your hike if inclement weather is predicted
- Wear a hat and sunscreen
- Wear hiking boots or sturdy walking shoes with good grip as the trails can be uneven and rocky
- Carry a first-aid kit, a fully charged cell phone (although many hiking trails do not have cell phone service), flashlight, compass, map, portable GPS unit, rescue whistle, pocketknife and a snack
- Hike with at least one other person and complete the hike before sunset
- If you must hike alone, let someone know where you'll be hiking and leave a note in your vehicle stating where you intend to hike and when you expect to return
- Trailhead parking areas can be the target of thieves so don't leave valuables in your vehicle
- Stay on the designated trail. Most rescues are for hikers who have left the trail to "explore"
- Downhill hikers have the right-of-way in most instances because footing is more tenuous downhill than uphill. If hiking uphill, step aside and let downhill hikers pass
- Bicyclists are supposed to yield to all trail users, but use common sense and step aside when appropriate
- There is no trash service in the forest. Take out anything you take in. "Take nothing but pictures, leave nothing but footprints"

Definition of the "Y"

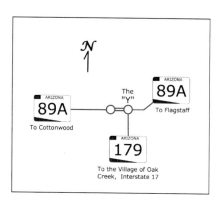

If you obtain directions from a Sedona local, chances are he or she will give you those directions referencing something called the "Y." We use the "Y" as our reference point in this guidebook also. The "Y" is the traffic circle at the intersection of State Route (SR) 89A and SR 179.

If you drive to Sedona from Flagstaff on SR 89A, the "Y" is the first of the two roundabouts you come to. And, if you drive to Sedona from Cottonwood, the "Y" is the second roundabout you enter, which is very close to the first roundabout.

Sedona Average Weather & Sunrise/Sunset Data

	Temperature (°F) High	Low	Precipitation (Inches)	Sunrise (1st of	Sunset Month)
January	56	30	2.10	7:32 AM	5:30 PM
February	60	33	2.16	7:24 AM	5:58 PM
March	65	37	2.47	6:57 AM	6:24 PM
April	73	42	1.16	6:16 AM	6:48 PM
May	82	49	0.71	5:40 AM	7:10 PM
June	93	58	0.36	5:19 AM	7:32 PM
July	97	64	1.65	5:21 AM	7:42 PM
August	94	63	1.90	5:40 AM	7:29 PM
September	88	58	1.94	6:02 AM	6:55 PM
October	77	48	1.67	6:22 AM	6:14 PM
November	64	36	1.38	6:46 AM	5:37 PM
December	57	31	1.51	7:14 AM	5:20 PM
Average	75	46	1.50		

Vortex Information

If you come to Sedona with the thought of visiting a vortex or two, you are not alone. It's estimated that more than half of Sedona visitors are interested in experiencing the power of vortexes (vortices). There are four main Sedona vortexes: Airport Mesa, Bell Rock, Boynton Canyon, and Cathedral Rock. All four locations are described in this guidebook. We suggest that you approach each vortex without preconceived ideas of what you may experience and just let the experience "happen." If nothing else, you'll enjoy some of Sedona's finest views. And, if you'd like additional information on the four main vortexes, plus information on the location of 10 additional "power spots" where vortex energy has been reported, you might be interested in our *Hiking the Vortexes* book that is available at many Sedona retailers, https://createspace.com/3538560 or scan the code below.

GPS Data

When you read the hike descriptions, you will find numbers in curly brackets such as {1}, {2} and so on. These numbers refer to the GPS waypoints in the maps below each of the hike descriptions. In addition, elevation data for each of the GPS coordinates are shown on the maps as well as cumulative ascent data (total distance you'll climb on the hike). Specific GPS data, including "tracks" in the universal gpx format for all the hikes contained in this guidebook are available at: http://greatsedonahikes.com/gps/gps.html.

Required Parking Pass

If you park in the National Forest around Sedona, you may need to display a Recreation Pass. If you park on private property or stop temporarily in the National Forest to take a photo remaining near your vehicle, you do not need to display a Recreation Pass.

A Recreation Pass is required for trailhead parking at many of the trails listed in this guide. [See pages 6 and 7, Alphabetical List of Included Hikes and look for this symbol **(RP)**.] It is also required for the Bootlegger, Banjo Bill, Halfway and Encinoso picnic areas in Oak Creek Canyon. Additionally, there are 3 special fee areas: Crescent Moon Ranch/Red Rock Crossing, West Fork Trail, and Grasshopper Point Picnic Area. Each area charges a separate, unique fee.

A Recreation Pass is: 1) A National Parks Pass, also known as a Federal Interagency Annual Pass 2) A Senior Pass, also known as a Federal Interagency Senior Pass issued to U.S. residents 62 years of age and older 3) A Federal Interagency Access Pass issued to individuals with permanent disabilities 4) A Red Rock Pass (described below).

If you do not have any of the above Federal Interagency Passes, you may display a Red Rock Pass, available for sale at many Sedona-area businesses, the Red Rock Ranger Station Visitor Center, the Sedona Chamber of Commerce Uptown Visitor Center and selected trailheads. The machines located at the trailheads only accept credit cards.

The Red Rock Pass is available as a $5 Daily Pass, a $15 Weekly Pass, a $20 Annual Pass, or a $40 Grand Annual Pass.

- The $5 Daily Red Rock Pass permits you to park in the National Forest as described above for the day of issue. It expires at midnight. It <u>does not include</u> the additional parking fees at the 3 special fee areas.
- The $15 Weekly Red Rock Pass permits you to park in the National Forest as described above for 7 days. It <u>does not include</u> the additional parking fees at the 3 special fee areas.
- The $20 Annual Red Rock Pass permits you to park in the National Forest as described above for 1 year. It <u>does not include</u> the additional parking fees at the 3 special fee areas.
- The $40 Grand Annual Pass permits you to park in the National Forest as described above and <u>includes</u> the additional parking fees at the 3 special fee areas for 1 year. It is available at the Red Rock Ranger Station and the Chamber's Uptown Visitor Center.

Because the Red Rock Pass Program changes periodically, check http://www.fs.usda.gov/main/coconino/passes-permits/recreation for the latest information.

Alphabetical List of Included Trails

List of Top 12 Trails

★ symbol indicates Favorite Trail. (RP) symbol indicates Recreation Pass required or Special Fee area. See page 7

Trails Rated by Level of Difficulty
Easy

Airport Vortex Trail
Bell Rock Vortex Trail
Boynton Canyon Vortex Trail ★
Fay Canyon Trail (not to arch) ★

Moderate

Airport Loop Trail
Baldwin Loop Trail ★
Bear Sign Trail
Bell Rock Loop Trail
Boynton Canyon Trail ★
Brins Mesa Overlook Trail ★
Broken Arrow Trail ★
Canyon of Fools Trail ★
Cibola Pass Trail
Courthouse Butte Loop Trail
Devil's Bridge Trail ★
Doe Mountain Trail ★
Dry Creek Trail
Fay Canyon Trail (to the arch) ★
HS Canyon Trail
Huckaby Trail
Jim Thompson Trail
Jordan Trail
Little Horse Trail ★
Llama Trail
Lost Canyon Trail
Mescal Trail
Pyramid Loop Trail
Soldier Pass Trail ★
Templeton Trail
West Fork Trail ★

Hard

Bear Mountain Trail ★
Cathedral Rock and Vortex Trail ★
Sterling Pass to Vultee Arch Trail

★ symbol indicates Favorite Trail

Trails By Feature

Trails To/Near Arches

Devil's Bridge Trail ★
Fay Canyon Trail ★
Soldier Pass Trail ★
Sterling Pass to Vultee Arch Trail

Indian Ruin Trails

Boynton Canyon Trail ★
Lost Canyon Trail

Vortex Trails

Airport Vortex Trail
Bell Rock Vortex Trail
Boynton Canyon Vortex Trail ★
Cathedral Rock Vortex Trail ★

Water Trails

Baldwin Loop Trail ★
Huckaby
Templeton Trail
West Fork Trail ★

Shaded Trails for Summer Hikes

The following trails provide partial shade and may be suitable for summer hiking. But be sure to take extra water when hiking in the summer.

Baldwin Loop Trail ★ (on the north and east side)
Bear Sign Trail
Boynton Canyon Trail ★ (past Enchantment Resort)
Cibola Pass Trail
Devil's Bridge Trail ★
Dry Creek
HS Canyon Trail
Sterling Pass Trail
West Fork Trail ★

Hikes for Muddy Trail Conditions

Baldwin Loop Trail ★
Boynton Canyon Trail ★
Courthouse Butte Loop Trail
Doe Mountain Trail ★
Fay Canyon Trail ★
Jim Thompson Trail
Little Horse Trail ★
Llama Trail
Templeton Trail

★ symbol indicates Favorite Trail

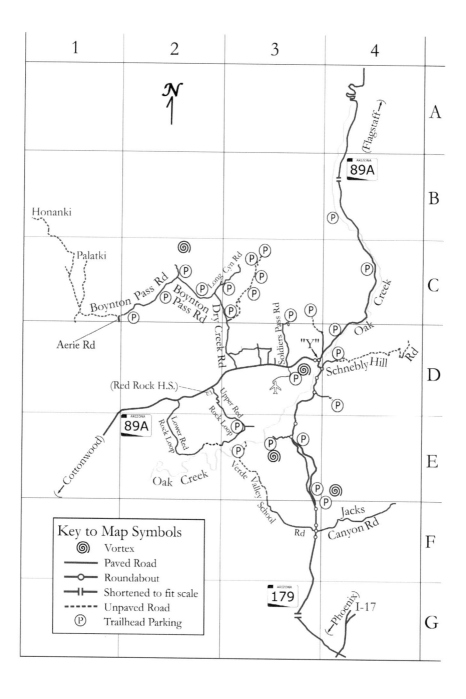

Airport Loop and Airport Vortex Trail

Summary: A loop hike that circles the Sedona Airport with nice views all around and a chance to visit one of Sedona's famous vortexes

Challenge Level: Easy for the vortex hike; Moderate for the loop hike

Hiking Distance: From the Airport Road parking area {1} less than 0.25 mile round trip for the vortex; about 3.3 miles for the loop hike, but add another 1.0 mile if you hike the Tabletop Trail. Add 1.2 miles to all the above mileages if you hike from the Sedona View parking area {2}.

Hiking Time: From the Airport Road parking area, about ½ hour round trip for the vortex; about 2 hours for the loop: add ½ hour for the Tabletop Trail. From the Sedona View parking area, add 1 hour to the above estimated hiking times

Trail Popularity: For the vortex: 🚶 🚶 🚶 🚶 For the loop hike: 🚶 🚶

Trailhead Directions: There are two ways to access this trail. From the "Y" roundabout (see page 5), drive west toward Cottonwood on SR 89A for 1.0 mile then turn left on Airport Road, which is the first traffic light west of the "Y." The primary trailhead is located approximately 0.5 mile up Airport Road on the left {1}. There is parking for 10 vehicles plus one handicapped spot here.

If the parking lot is full, continue for 0.6 mile then turn left into the Scenic View parking area. You'll find the Sedona View trailhead at the northeast corner of the parking area {2}.

Description: If you park on Airport Road {1}, you can easily reach one of Sedona's famous vortexes. From the parking area continue past the first sign then follow the main trail east until you come to a second sign in about 200 feet {3}. Turn left here then follow the trail to "Overlook Point" for a short distance then make a right turn to climb up about 50 feet to the overlook. The top of the rock formation is "Overlook Point" and is considered to be the vortex {4}. (Additional information on vortexes can be found on page 6.) From the Scenic View parking area {2}, hike the Scenic View Trail for 0.6 mile. Continue past the intersection with the Airport Loop Trail to the intersection with the sign for "Overlook Point" {3} to go to the vortex {4}.

As you hike around Airport Mesa below the Sedona Airport, there are good views all around. On the east, there are great views of Twin Buttes and, to the south, Cathedral Rock. Be sure to hike the 0.5 mile Tabletop Trail at the southwest end of the runway {5} to the end of the mesa {6} for a spectacular view of Sedona's pyramid. Return to the Airport Loop Trail where after 0.6 mile you'll intersect the Bandit Trail {7} and have nice views of Chimney Rock, Capitol Butte and Coffeepot Rock on the north side of the loop.

Note: Don't attempt this rock-strewn trail if a narrow trail and steep drop-offs are a concern. The trail is very rocky and twisted ankles are a common occurrence.

More Photos: Scan the QR code for more photos of this trail

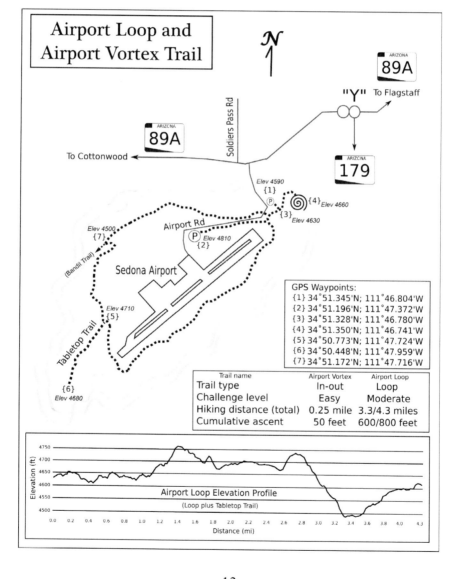

Baldwin Loop Trail ★

Summary: This loop trail at the base of Cathedral Rock offers some excellent views with an optional short side trip to the banks of Oak Creek

Challenge Level: Moderate

Hiking Distance: About a 2.7 mile loop

Hiking Time: About 1½ hours round trip

Trail Popularity:

Trailhead Directions: The trailhead is located on the unpaved portion of Verde Valley School Road. From the "Y" roundabout (see page 5), drive south on SR 179 about 7 miles to the Jacks Canyon and Verde Valley School Road roundabout then turn right (west) on to Verde Valley School Road. At 4 miles you'll pass the Turkey Creek parking area on your left {10} and at 4.5 miles you'll see the Baldwin Trail parking area on the left (west) side of Verde Valley School Road {1}. The trailhead is across the road from the north end of the parking area. There are toilets at the parking area.

Description: Named for Andrew Baldwin, one of the individuals who bought Crescent Moon Ranch in 1936, the Baldwin Loop Trail circles an unnamed red rock butte beside Cathedral Rock providing excellent panoramic views of Cathedral Rock. After crossing the road, you'll come to a signboard {2}. You can hike the Baldwin Trail in either direction. If you hike in the clockwise direction, you'll intersect an unmarked "social trail" in 0.3 mile {3} and the Templeton Trail after 0.5 mile {4}. Take a side trip by hiking east on the Templeton Trail until it goes beside Oak Creek. After 0.2 mile, look across Oak Creek to see "Buddha Beach," where visitors use river rock to build amazing stacked structures {5}. Periodically, floods knock the structures down, but they are usually quickly rebuilt. You may be lucky and see hundreds of "buddhas." If you continue east on the Templeton Trail for 0.8 mile, you'll intersect the Cathedral Rock Trail.

Return to the Baldwin Loop Trail intersection then turn left to continue around the tall red rock butte. You'll pass some excellent places to stop and enjoy the views {6}{8} on your loop. You'll intersect the HiLine Trail {7}, which is a popular mountain biking trail, and a spur off of the Baldwin Loop Trail {9} that leads across Verde Valley School Road to the Turkey Creek Trail parking area {10}. For the best photos of Cathedral Rock, do this hike later in the day.

More Photos: Scan the QR code for more photos of this trail

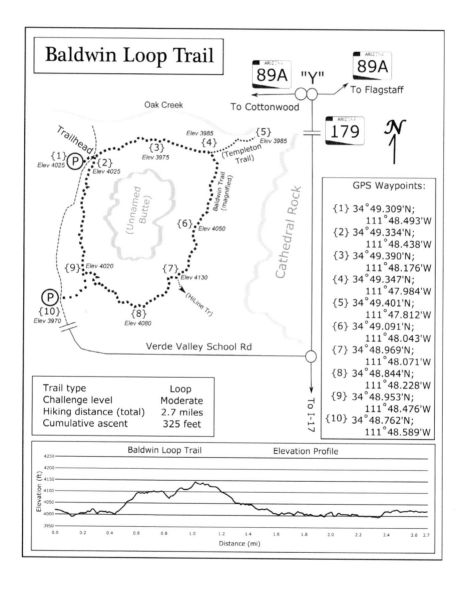

Bear Mountain Trail ★

Summary: A strenuous, sunny, in-out hike with excellent red rock views

Challenge Level: Hard

Hiking Distance: To the top of Bear Mountain is about 2.4 miles each way or 4.8 miles round trip

Hiking Time: About 4 hours round trip

Trail Popularity:

Trailhead Directions: From the "Y" roundabout (see page 5), drive west toward Cottonwood on SR 89A about 3 miles. Turn right on Dry Creek Road (where speed limits are strictly enforced). Stay on Dry Creek Road to a stop sign (about 3 miles) then turn left on Boynton Pass Road. Proceed about 1.6 miles to a stop sign. Turn left and continue on Boynton Pass Road. Trailhead parking {1} is shared with Doe Mountain Trail and is the second parking area on the left side, about 1.75 miles from the stop sign. The Bear Mountain Trail begins across the road from the parking area. There are toilets at the parking area.

Description: Bear Mountain provides fantastic views of Doe Mountain (and beyond) and nearby canyons. You'll be hiking up with a cumulative ascent of some 2100 feet. This makes Bear Mountain a hard hike.

After crossing the road and crawling through the gate, you first cross a series of three deep washes and enter a meadow-like landscape. After 0.3 mile, you begin the climb up the mountain. Throughout the hike, be sure to look around to enjoy the great views. After 0.6 mile you'll come to a huge rock beside the trail {2}.

At 1.2 mile you'll come to a flat area {3} and soon have to scramble up in a narrow slot. At 1.4 miles, you'll reach a summit {4} then begin a series of descents and ascents. At 2.0 miles, you'll come to a large area of slickrock {5}, soon followed by a natural stopping place and photo opportunity at elevation 6150 feet {6}.

To reach the very top of Bear Mountain, you'll hike an additional 0.4 mile with ascents and descents. From the top of Bear Mountain {7}, look north and you can see the San Francisco Peaks northwest of Flagstaff.

Note: The trail is fairly well-marked by cairns placed by other hikers. The trail is rocky with exposed and extreme drop-offs in some parts – watch your footing.

More Photos: Scan the QR code for more photos of this trail

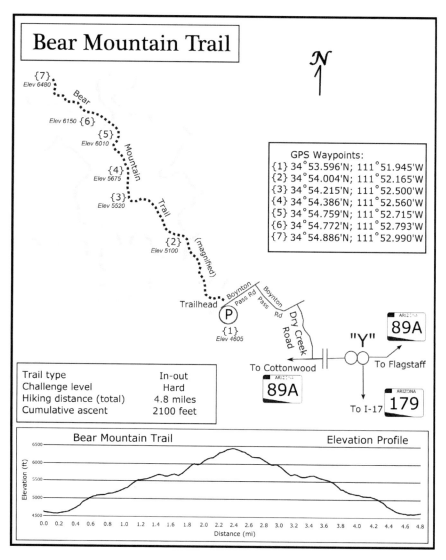

Bear Sign Trail

Summary: A beautiful, in-out hike in a forested red rock canyon

Challenge Level: Moderate

Hiking Distance: About 3 miles each way or 6 miles round trip

Hiking Time: About 4 hours round trip

Trail Popularity:

Trailhead Directions: From the "Y" roundabout (see page 5), drive west toward Cottonwood on SR 89A about 3 miles. Turn right on Dry Creek Road (where speed limits are strictly enforced). Stay on Dry Creek Road for 2 miles then turn right on Forest Road (FR) 152. Proceed to the end of FR 152 (about 4.5 miles) to the parking area on the left {1}. The parking area is the same as used for the Dry Creek and Vultee Arch Trails.

Note: FR 152 is an extremely rough road beyond the 0.2 mile paved section; a high clearance vehicle is necessary and 4WD is recommended.

Description: This trail is seldom used because it is difficult to get to. As a result the trail will likely be somewhat overgrown with logs and other obstacles you must navigate.

After you park, proceed in a northwesterly direction on the Dry Creek Trail. You'll be hiking in the forest so there is shade. The trail is relatively flat at the start then begins a gentle climb. After about 0.6 mile, you'll come to a fork where the Dry Creek Trail goes to the right and the Bear Sign Trail begins to the left {2}. Grizzly bears reportedly roamed the area until the 1930s; you may actually see signs of black bear along the trail.

Hike some 2.8 miles to the intersection of the David Miller Trail {3}. A short, but steep hike up the David Miller Trail about 0.2 mile provides a lovely view from the saddle of the ridge between Bear Sign and Secret Canyons {4}.

More Photos: Scan the QR code for more photos of this trail

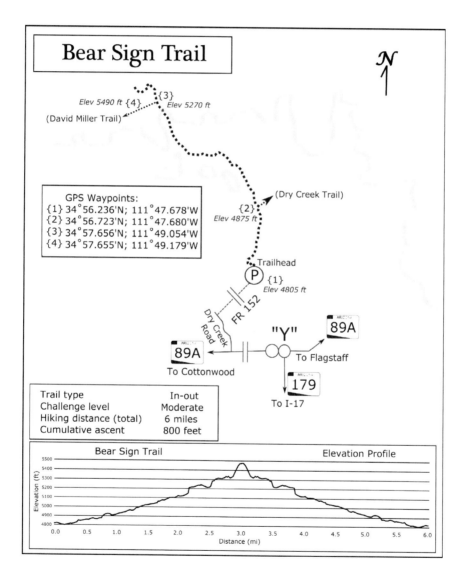

Bell Rock Loop and
Bell Rock Vortex Trail

Summary: Explore the north side of Bell Rock on this in-out hike where you may experience some vortex energy then hike a loop around Bell Rock

Challenge Level: Easy for the vortex hike; Moderate for the loop hike

Hiking Distance: About 1/2 mile each way or 1 mile round trip to experience the Bell Rock Vortex; 2.3 miles to make a loop hike

Hiking Time: About 45 minutes round trip for the vortex hike; about 1 ¾ hours round trip for the loop hike

Trail Popularity: 🚶🚶 🚶🚶 🚶🚶 🚶🚶

Trailhead Directions: From the "Y" roundabout (see page 5), drive south on SR 179 for about 5 miles to the parking area. After you drive about 3.2 miles, just past the Back O' Beyond roundabout, SR 179 becomes a divided highway. Continue driving south. About 1.8 miles beyond the Back O' Beyond roundabout, southbound SR 179 adds a passing lane on the left. From the passing lane, turn left at the sign for the "Court House Vista" parking area {1} (it's the second scenic view on the left side of SR 179). Before you turn, you'll see Bell Rock ahead of you on the left side of SR 179. There are toilets at the parking area. The trail starts on the southeast side of the parking area.

Description: After you park in the Court House Vista parking area, walk past the interpretive signboard then proceed straight ahead on the Bell Rock Trail. Follow it for 0.2 mile to the intersection with the Bell Rock Pathway (BRP) Trail {2}. From here you can continue straight ahead on the Bell Rock Climb to explore the northeast side of Bell Rock. To hike a loop around Bell Rock, turn right and follow the BRP Trail south for just under 0.1 mile to the intersection with the Phone Trail.

If you want to climb up to a vortex area known as the Meditation Perch, look to the left for a series of cairns going up on to Bell Rock {3}. (Additional information on vortexes can be found on page 6.) Follow the cairns until you reach the 10th cairn then turn right {4}. Go across the slickrock area and you'll see the Meditation Perch ahead {5}. After your vortex experience, return to the BRP Trail {3} then turn left. Follow the BRP Trail for 0.4 mile then turn left on to the Courthouse Butte Loop Trail {6}. Follow it for 0.25 mile then turn left (north) on an unmarked trail which goes between Bell Rock and Courthouse Butte {7}. Soon you'll go past a fence {8}. Continue on another 0.5 mile and keep left at the fork in the trail {9}. You'll shortly intersect the BRP Trail {10}. Turn left and in 0.2 mile you'll intersect the Bell Rock Trail on the right {2} back to the parking area {1}.

More Photos: Scan the QR code for more photos of this trail

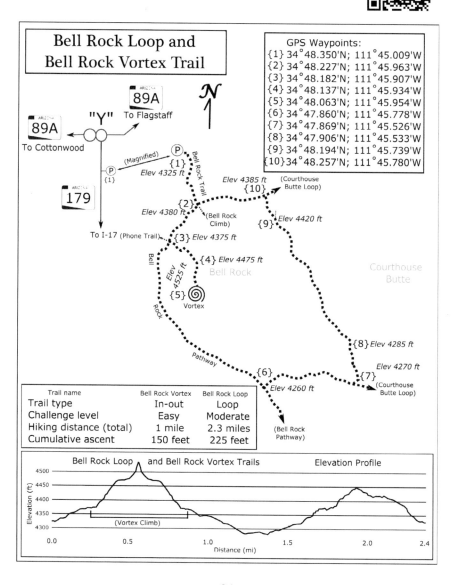

Bell Rock Loop and Bell Rock Vortex Trail

GPS Waypoints:
{1} 34°48.350'N; 111°45.009'W
{2} 34°48.227'N; 111°45.963'W
{3} 34°48.182'N; 111°45.907'W
{4} 34°48.137'N; 111°45.934'W
{5} 34°48.063'N; 111°45.954'W
{6} 34°47.860'N; 111°45.778'W
{7} 34°47.869'N; 111°45.526'W
{8} 34°47.906'N; 111°45.533'W
{9} 34°48.194'N; 111°45.739'W
{10} 34°48.257'N; 111°45.780'W

Trail name	Bell Rock Vortex	Bell Rock Loop
Trail type	In-out	Loop
Challenge level	Easy	Moderate
Hiking distance (total)	1 mile	2.3 miles
Cumulative ascent	150 feet	225 feet

Bell Rock Loop and Bell Rock Vortex Trails — Elevation Profile

Boynton Canyon and
Boynton Vortex Trail ★

Summary: An in-out hike to a famous Sedona vortex area then into a forested canyon with nice red rock views

Challenge Level: Easy for the vortex hike; Moderate for the canyon hike

Hiking Distance: About 1 ¼ miles round trip to the vortex; about 3.2 miles each way or 6.4 miles round trip for the canyon hike

Hiking Time: About 1 hour round trip to the vortex; about 3 hours round trip for the canyon hike

Trail Popularity:

Trailhead Directions: From the "Y" roundabout (see page 5), drive west toward Cottonwood on SR 89A about 3 miles. Turn right on Dry Creek Road (where speed limits are strictly enforced). Stay on Dry Creek Road to a stop sign (about 3 miles) then turn left on Boynton Pass Road. Proceed about 1.6 miles to a stop sign. Turn right, the trailhead parking is about 0.1 mile on the right {1}. There are toilets at the parking area.

Description: Boynton Canyon was named for John Boeington, who was a horse rancher in the canyon around 1886. Boynton Canyon is a very popular hike. The nicest part of the hike is located beyond the Enchantment Resort. We like it for its summer shade and good red rock views. It is also a well-known vortex site. After hiking about 0.25 mile from the parking area, you'll see a sign for the Boynton Vista Trail to the right {2}. Hike the Vista Trail for about 0.4 mile slightly uphill to two tall rock formations, both of which are considered vortex points {3}. (Additional information on vortexes can be found on page 6.)

After visiting the vortexes, return to the Boynton Canyon Trail then continue to the north. The trail beside the Enchantment Resort is rocky and narrow, and is the most difficult part of the trail. Once you are past the Enchantment Resort, the trail widens and follows the canyon floor.

Just after you come to the end of the Enchantment Resort property, you can see evidence of prior habitation on the right {4}. Soon you'll enter a forest where the trail and views are excellent, although some of the views are blocked by the trees. You'll see some nice fall colors usually during the third week of October about 2 miles from the trailhead. The trail ends in a box canyon after a steep climb at the base of Secret Mountain {5}.

More Photos: Scan the QR code for more photos of this trail

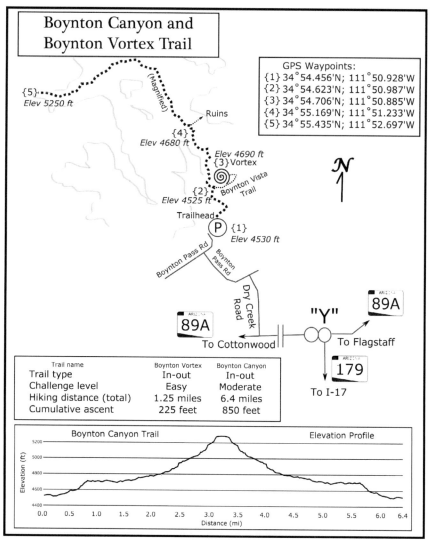

Boynton Canyon and Boynton Vortex Trail

GPS Waypoints:
{1} 34°54.456'N; 111°50.928'W
{2} 34°54.623'N; 111°50.987'W
{3} 34°54.706'N; 111°50.885'W
{4} 34°55.169'N; 111°51.233'W
{5} 34°55.435'N; 111°52.697'W

{5}
Elev 5250 ft

(Magnified)

Ruins

{4}
Elev 4680 ft

Elev 4690 ft
{3} Vortex

Boynton Vista Trail

{2}
Elev 4525 ft

N

Trailhead

P {1}
Elev 4530 ft

Boynton Pass Rd

Boynton Pass Rd

Dry Creek Road

89A

"Y"

89A

To Cottonwood

To Flagstaff

179

To I-17

Trail name	Boynton Vortex	Boynton Canyon
Trail type	In-out	In-out
Challenge level	Easy	Moderate
Hiking distance (total)	1.25 miles	6.4 miles
Cumulative ascent	225 feet	850 feet

Boynton Canyon Trail — Elevation Profile

Brins Mesa Overlook Trail ★

Summary: A hike up to a beautiful mesa then on to a knoll with red rock views all around.

Challenge Level: Moderate

Hiking Distance: About 1.5 miles each way to the top of Brins Mesa or 3 miles round trip; add 0.7 mile one way to the overlook or 4.4 miles round trip

Hiking Time: About 2 1/2 hours round trip

Trail Popularity: 🚶🚶 🚶🚶

Trailhead Directions: From the "Y" roundabout (see page 5), drive north on SR 89A about 0.3 mile to Jordan Road. Turn left on Jordan Road then drive to the end. Turn left on West Park Ridge Drive then proceed through the paved cul-de-sac, continuing on the dirt road for 0.5 mile to the parking area {1}. There are toilets at the parking area.

Description: The trail begins on the west side of the parking area and as you begin the hike up to Brins Mesa, you are rewarded with some outstanding views. You'll be hiking up about 550 feet to reach the edge of the mesa. The trail becomes much steeper as you approach it. Immediately after you reach the mesa {2}, look for a faint trail to your right. You'll follow this trail for 0.2 mile and bear left at a fork in the trail {3}. If you go right, you'll shortly come to a scenic outcropping of red rock, which has a nice view {4}. As you continue along the

24

left fork, the trail continues to gently rise then narrows as it follows the north side of Brins Mesa. You'll soon see the overlook ahead. A moderate amount of scrambling is needed to reach the top of the knoll, but the climb is well worth the effort. Once on top, there is a spectacular view overlooking Mormon Canyon {5}. Look high up on the rock face to the southeast. If you are lucky, that's where you may see Angel Falls flowing with the spring snow melt.

More Photos: Scan the QR code for more photos of this trail

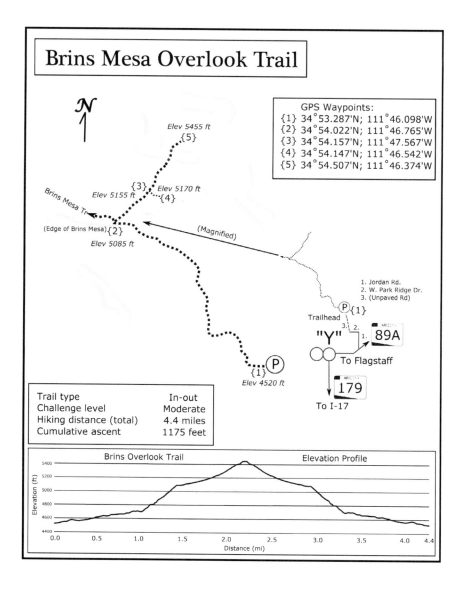

Brins Mesa Overlook Trail

Elev 5455 ft
{5}

GPS Waypoints:
{1} 34°53.287'N; 111°46.098'W
{2} 34°54.022'N; 111°46.765'W
{3} 34°54.157'N; 111°47.567'W
{4} 34°54.147'N; 111°46.542'W
{5} 34°54.507'N; 111°46.374'W

{3} Elev 5170 ft
Brins Mesa Tr   Elev 5155 ft   {4}

(Edge of Brins Mesa) {2}   (Magnified)
Elev 5085 ft

1. Jordan Rd.
2. W. Park Ridge Dr.
3. (Unpaved Rd)

P {1}
Trailhead
3. 2.
"Y"   1.   89A

To Flagstaff

{1} P
Elev 4520 ft

179

To I-17

Trail type	In-out
Challenge level	Moderate
Hiking distance (total)	4.4 miles
Cumulative ascent	1175 feet

Brins Overlook Trail   Elevation Profile

Elevation (ft)

5400
5200
5000
4800
4600
4400
0.0   0.5   1.0   1.5   2.0   2.5   3.0   3.5   4.0 4.4
Distance (mi)

Broken Arrow Trail ★

Summary: A sunny, picturesque in-out trip to Devil's Dining Room and Chicken Point with a side trip to Submarine Rock

Challenge Level: Moderate

Hiking Distance: About 1.5 miles each way to Chicken Point or 3 miles round trip; about 4 miles round trip if you hike the loop to Submarine Rock then Chicken Point and return

Hiking Time: About 2 hours round trip

Trail Popularity: 🚶🚶🚶🚶

Trailhead Directions: From the "Y" roundabout (see page 5), drive south on SR 179 for 1.5 miles to the roundabout at Morgan Road. Turn left (east) on Morgan Road then drive about 0.6 mile (the last part is a dirt road) to the trailhead parking on your left {1}. There is room for about 25 vehicles in and around the parking area.

Description: The trail is named for the movie, *Broken Arrow*, which was filmed in the area in 1950. From the parking area, go south across the jeep road to the trail. Initially, the trail essentially parallels the jeep road. You'll intersect the Twin Buttes Trail after 0.2 mile. After hiking about 0.4 mile, watch for a fence on the right which surrounds a sinkhole known as the Devil's Dining Room {2}. As you continue along the trail, after about another 0.4 mile you'll come to a sign and a fork in the trail {3}. Continue on the Broken Arrow Trail for another 0.7 mile to Chicken Point or turn left to go to Submarine Rock.

Submarine rock is a very large rock formation with panoramic views all around. While you can scramble up on the north end, we prefer to hike around to the south end where it is easy to get on the top of Submarine Rock. To get to Chicken Point from the south end of Submarine Rock, look down and you'll see where the Pink Jeeps park. Go down to that parking area and follow the jeep road southwest. Be sure to stay out of the way of the jeeps as you hike along this narrow road.

Chicken Point is named for thrill-seeking jeep drivers who once dared to drive close to the edge of the point (jeep access is no longer permitted on Chicken

Point). If you look to the south, you'll see a "chicken-shaped" rock high up on the red rock cliff. Chicken Point is a nice place for a snack break as the views are outstanding {5}. You'll likely encounter some Pink Jeeps as the "Broken Arrow" tour brings many visitors to this beautiful area.

More Photos: Scan the QR code for more photos of this trail

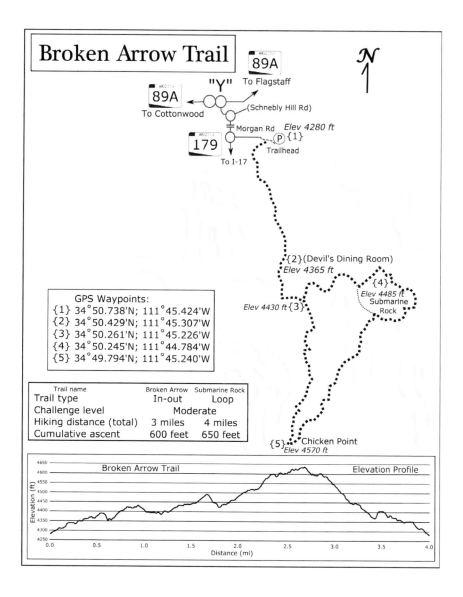

Canyon of Fools Trail ★

Summary: An in-out or loop hike that provides great red rock views of Mescal Mountain

Challenge Level: Moderate

Hiking Distance: About a 2.6 mile in-out hike or a 3 mile loop

Hiking Time: About 1 ½ hours round trip for the in-out hike; about 2 hours for the loop hike

Trail Popularity: 👫

Trailhead Directions: From the "Y" roundabout (see page 5), drive west toward Cottonwood on SR 89A about 3 miles. Turn right on Dry Creek Road (where speed limits are strictly enforced). Stay on Dry Creek Road to a stop sign (about 3 miles) then turn left on Boynton Pass Road. Proceed about 0.6 mile to a small unmarked parking area on the right {1}. There is room for about 4 vehicles here on the north side of Boynton Pass Road and about 4 more vehicles on the south side (where the Dawa Trail begins). The trail begins on the north side of the road.

Description: Shortly beyond the trail marker, turn right and follow a narrow canyon with high walls for about 0.4 mile. This is the "Fools" part of the canyon. You'll note that the mountain bikers sometimes take a path parallel to the canyon but you should try to stay in the wash. As you continue north, you'll intersect the Yucca Trail after 0.5 mile and begin to have excellent views of Mescal Mountain ahead {2}. Turn left (north) here to continue on the Canyon of Fools Trail. You'll soon be in a forest of Junipers and Pinon Pines and come to a nice spot for a break at 1.1 miles {3}. You'll intersect the Mescal Trail after 1.3 miles {4}. Return the same way for a 2.6 mile hike.

If you want to hike a loop, turn right at {4} and follow the Mescal Trail. This part of the Mescal Trail provides wonderful up-close views of Mescal Mountain. After 0.7 mile, turn right on to the Yucca Trail {5}. You have great panoramic views of Mescal Mountain for the first 0.3 mile. Follow the Yucca Trail for 0.4 mile to the intersection with the Canyon of Fools Trail {2}. Turn left (south) here and follow the Canyon of Fools Trail back to the parking area for a 3 mile hike.

Note: Do not hike the Canyon of Fools Trail after a hard rain as the narrow canyon may be filled with fast moving water. Also, stay alert for mountain bikers in front of and behind you in the "Fools" part of the canyon because it is very narrow in places and there are several blind corners.

More Photos: Scan the QR code for more photos of this trail

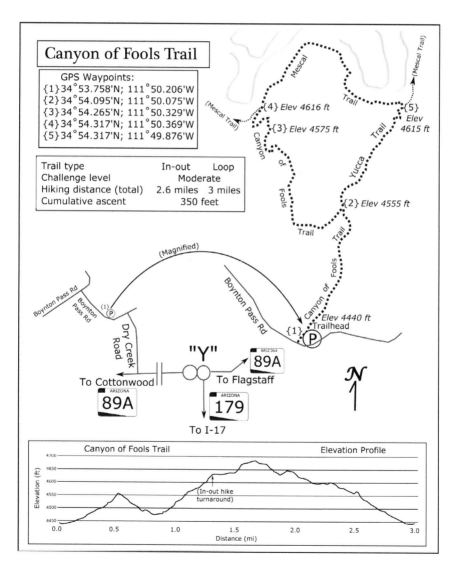

Cathedral Rock and Cathedral Vortex Trail

Summary: A steep, sunny in-out hike to the "saddle" of Cathedral Rock for spectacular views all around and the location of one of Sedona's famous vortex sites

Challenge Level: Hard

Hiking Distance: About 0.75 miles each way or 1.5 miles round trip

Hiking Time: About 1 ½ hour round trip

Trail Popularity: 🚶🚶🚶

Trailhead Directions: From the "Y" roundabout (see page 5), drive south on SR 179 about 3.2 miles to the Back O' Beyond roundabout. Turn right then go west on the Back O' Beyond Road for about 0.75 mile. The parking area is on your left {1}. If the parking area is full, see the Baldwin Loop Trail or HT Trail description.

Description: If you want to get up close and personal with Cathedral Rock, this short, strenuous hike is for you. The trail begins on the right (west) side of the parking area on Back 'O Beyond Road.. You'll start out crossing a dry creek bed. Continue climbing up until the trail intersects the Templeton Trail {2}. Turn right then go about 60 paces to the branching off of the Cathedral Rock Trail on your left {3}.

From here, the trail becomes very steep. Good hiking boots or other footwear with good traction is recommended. Once you arrive at the saddle of Cathedral

Rock {4}, you are at the location of one of four main vortex sites in Sedona. (Additional information on vortexes can be found on page 6.)

There are short trails along the south side of the east and west rock formations that lead to some good views, although the footing can be tricky.

Note: If heights, an extremely steep trail or tenuous footing bothers you, or the trail is wet or snowy (making it slippery), we do not recommend this trail.

More Photos: Scan the QR code for more photos of this trail

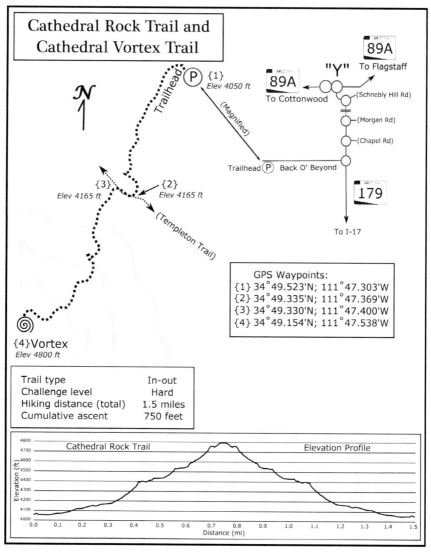

Cibola Pass Trail

Summary:
This close-to-town, in-out hike provides some spectacular red rock views with the option to hike a loop, visit the Devil's Kitchen sinkhole and the Seven Sacred Pools

Challenge Level:
Moderate

Hiking Distance: About 0.75 mile each way or 1.5 miles round trip; about a 2 mile loop if you hike the Cibola Pass Trail then return on the Jordan Trail; about 3.6 miles loop if you hike the Cibola Pass Trail to the Jordan Trail to the Soldier Pass Trail to the Seven Sacred Pools returning via the Jordan Trail

Hiking Time: About 1 ½ hour round trip for the Cibola-Jordan loop; about 2 ½ hours round trip to the Seven Sacred Pools and return

Trail Popularity: 🚶🚶🚶

Trailhead Directions: From the "Y" roundabout (see page 5), drive north on SR 89A about 0.3 mile to Jordan Road. Turn left on Jordan Road then drive to the end. Turn left on West Park Ridge Drive then proceed through the paved cul-de-sac, continuing on the dirt road for 0.5 mile to the parking area {1}. There are toilets at the parking area.

Description: Begin hiking the trail on the west side of the parking area near the toilets. Go through the opening in the cable fence. The Cibola Pass Trail branches left from the Brins Mesa Trail after about 400 feet {2}. The trail is quite steep in places. As you proceed, you'll have some very nice red rock views. At about 0.4 mile, you'll approach two fence posts on the left side {3}. If you go straight for a short distance, you'll have some great views. Return to the fence posts then continue on the trail. You'll meet the Jordan Trail after hiking 0.75 mile {4}. Turn around here to return to the parking area via the Cibola Trail, or turn south and follow the Jordan Trail back to the parking area for a 2 mile loop.

Or proceed west on the Jordan Trail for 0.4 mile to the Soldier Pass Trail. Turn right on the Soldier Pass Trail, which leads to Devil's Kitchen (a very large sink hole) {5}. Continue on the Soldier Pass Trail for 0.4 mile and you'll arrive at the Seven Sacred Pools {6}. You'll have hiked about 3.6 miles for the entire hike from the Seven Sacred Pools when you return to the parking area via the Jordan Trail.

More Photos: Scan the QR code for more photos of this trail

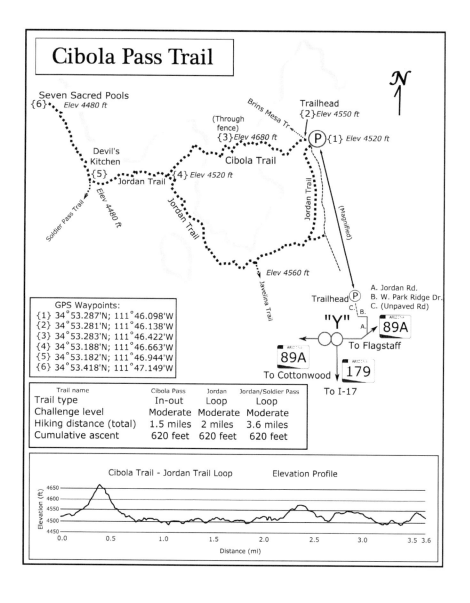

Courthouse Butte Loop Trail

Summary: A pleasant loop hike circling Bell Rock and Courthouse Butte near the Village of Oak Creek

Challenge Level: Moderate

Hiking Distance: About 4.2 miles loop

Hiking Time: About 2 ½ hours round trip

Trail Popularity: 👫👫👫

Trailhead Directions: There are two parking areas you can use for this hike. From the "Y" roundabout (see page 5), drive south on SR 179 for about 5 miles to the first parking area. After you drive about 3.2 miles, just past the Back O' Beyond roundabout, SR 179 becomes a divided highway. Continue driving south. About 1.8 miles beyond the Back O' Beyond roundabout, southbound SR 179 adds a passing lane on the left. From the passing lane, turn left at the sign for the "Court House Vista" parking area {1} (it's the second scenic view on the left side of SR 179).

Before you turn, you'll see Bell Rock ahead of you on the left side of SR 179. The trail starts on the southeast side of the parking area. After you park, walk past the interpretive signboard then proceed straight ahead on the Bell Rock Trail. Follow it for 0.1 mile to the intersection with the Courthouse Butte Loop Trail {2}.

If you continue driving south on SR 179, in 1 mile you'll come to the "Bell Rock Vista," the second parking area, on your left. Turn left into the parking area {8}. There are toilets at both the parking areas. Follow the Bell Rock Pathway Trail north for about 0.5 mile until you intersect the Courthouse Butte Loop Trail {7}.

Description: This trail circling Courthouse Butte and Bell Rock combines panoramic and close-up views of these two famous rock formations as well as distant views of Rabbit Ears, the Chapel of the Holy Cross and Cathedral Rock. The trail is fairly open, so it provides limited shade making it a hot summer hike.

We like to hike this loop in the clockwise direction from the Bell Rock Vista parking area, although either direction provides great views. You'll intersect several trails as you hike including the Llama Trail {3} and Big Park Loop Trail

{5}. From the Bell Rock Vista parking area, the trail starts out wide and defined by fences on both sides. A good stopping point for a snack break is near "Muffin Rock," which some call "UFO Rock" {4}.

More Photos: Scan the QR code for more photos of this trail

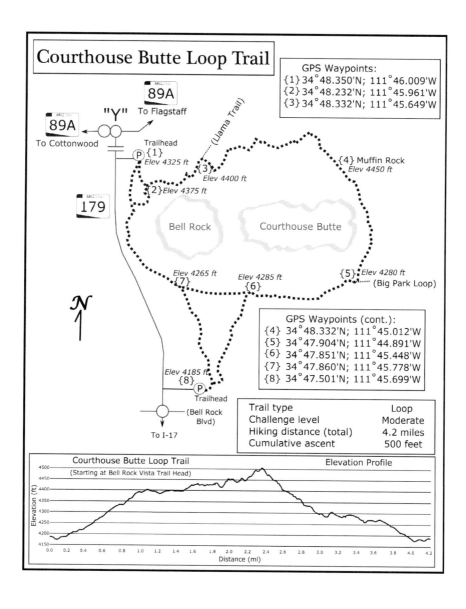

Devil's Bridge Trail ★

Summary: A moderate in-out climb with steep "stairs" up to the largest natural stone arch in the Sedona area

Challenge Level: Moderate

Hiking Distance: About 1 mile each way From the Devil's Bridge (DB) parking area or 2 miles round trip; about 2.2 miles each way from the Mescal Trail parking area or 4.4 miles round trip; about 3.1 miles each way from the Dry Creek Vista parking area or 6.2 miles round trip

Hiking Time: About 1½ hour round trip from the DB parking area; about 2 ½ hours round trip from the Mescal Trail parking area; about 3 ½ hours round trip from the Dry Creek Vista parking area

Trail Popularity: 🚶🚶🚶🚶

Trailhead Directions: From the "Y" roundabout (see page 5), drive west toward Cottonwood on SR 89A about 3 miles. Turn right on Dry Creek Road (where speed limits are strictly enforced). Stay on Dry Creek Road for about 2 miles then turn right on Forest Road (FR) 152. Drive for 0.2 mile and park at the Dry Creek Vista parking area {1}. If you have a high clearance vehicle, proceed for another 1.1 miles on the unpaved, very rough FR 152 to the DB parking area on your right {2}. Or rather than turn on to FR 152, a third alternative is to continue on Dry Creek Road another 1 mile then turn right on Long Canyon Road. Drive 0.3 mile to the Mescal Trail parking area on the right {3}.

Note: FR 152 is an extremely rough road beyond the 0.2 mile paved section; a high clearance vehicle is necessary and 4WD is recommended.

Description: From the Dry Creek Vista parking area, go to the signboard where you'll see a small sign pointing to the right for the Chuck Wagon (CW) Trail. As you hike CW, you'll pass the intersection of the trail to the Mescal Trail parking area {3} after 1.1 miles {4}. Continue on the CW Trail for a total of 2.1 miles then turn right on the connector trail to the DB parking area across FR 152 {5}.

For most folks, we recommend starting from the Mescal Trail parking area {3}. Hike the connector trail from the northeast end of the parking area for 0.2 mile then turn left on the CW Trail {4}. Hike for 0.8 mile to the turn to DB {5}.

Devil's Bridge is a large natural stone arch that you can walk on. It is reachable with a moderate amount of climbing (up some 400 feet); the view of the arch

Note: The unmarked, unmaintained trail is difficult to follow at times. We strongly recommend using a portable GPS unit to hike around the top of Doe Mountain and back to the trail to the parking area (go to http://greatsedonahikes.com/gps/gps.html).

More Photos: Scan the QR code for more photos of this trail

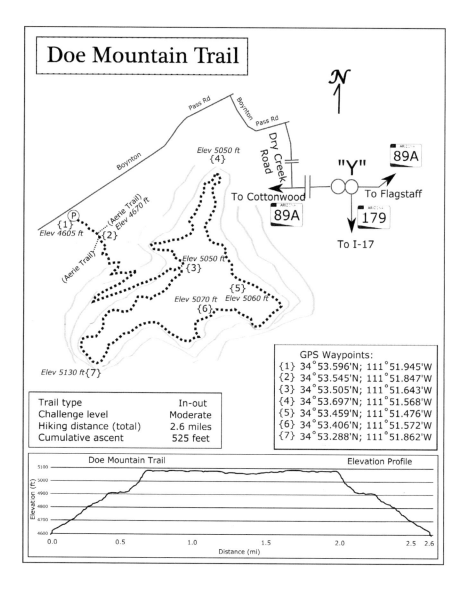

Dry Creek Trail

Summary: An in-out hike that follows the path of Dry Creek through a forest

Challenge Level: Easy to Moderate, depending on length of hike

Hiking Distance: About 2.25 miles each way or 4.5 miles round trip

Hiking Time: About 2 ½ hours round trip

Trail Popularity: 🏃

Trailhead Directions: From the "Y" roundabout (see page 5), drive west toward Cottonwood on SR 89A about 3 miles. Turn right on Dry Creek Road (where speed limits are strictly enforced). Stay on Dry Creek Road for 2 miles then turn right on Forest Road (FR) 152. Proceed to the end of FR 152 (about 4.5 miles) to the parking area on the left {1}. The parking area is the same as used for the Bear Sign and Vultee Arch Trails.

Note: FR 152 is an extremely rough road beyond the 0.2 mile paved section; a high clearance vehicle is necessary and 4WD is recommended.

Description: This trail, which is at the northern edge of the Red Rock-Secret Mountain Wilderness, follows the path cut by Dry Creek, crossing the dry creek bed about a dozen times. Because it is located at the end of the very rough FR 152, it isn't used very much and has become hard to follow in certain spots. We recommend you use a GPS loaded with the trail data (go to http://greatsedonahikes.com/gps/gps.html).

You'll be hiking in a northerly direction and intersect the Bear Sign Trail about 0.75 mile from the parking area {2}. The Dry Creek Trail is easy to follow here

40

but pay attention when you cross the creek bed because the continuation of the trail on the other side isn't always obvious. As you continue, the canyon cut by Dry Creek gets narrower and you are treated to nice views of towering red rock formations, although some of the views are blocked by the stands of cypress and pines {3}. You'll come to a nice place for a snack after about 1.6 miles {4}. You can hike another 0.75 mile further up the creek bed if you like {5} but the trail becomes harder and harder to follow.

More Photos: Scan the QR code for more photos of this trail

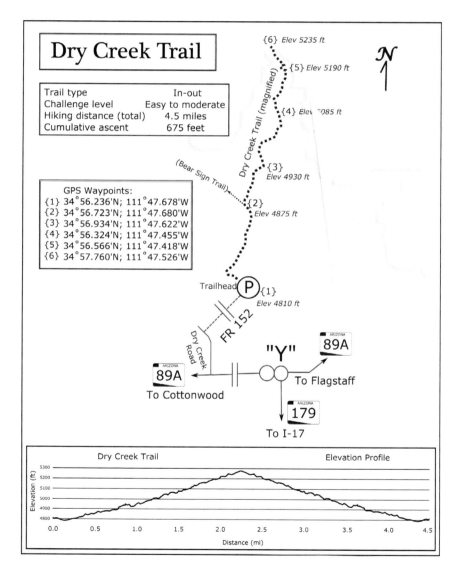

Fay Canyon Trail ★

Summary: A short, pleasant in-out stroll through a canyon with wonderful red rock views and an optional side trip to view a natural arch

Challenge Level: Easy for the Fay Canyon Trail; Moderate if you hike to Fay Canyon Arch

Hiking Distance: About 1.1 miles each way to the rock slide or 2.2 miles round trip. Add 0.5 mile round trip if you hike to Fay Canyon Arch or 2.7 miles round trip.

Hiking Time: About 1 ½ hours round trip

Trail Popularity: 🚶🚶🚶🚶

Trailhead Directions: From the "Y" roundabout (see page 5), drive west toward Cottonwood on SR 89A about 3 miles. Turn right on Dry Creek Road (where speed limits are strictly enforced). Stay on Dry Creek Road to a stop sign (about 3 miles) then turn left on Boynton Pass Road. Proceed about 1.6 miles to a stop sign. Turn left, continuing on Boynton Pass Road. You park at the first parking area on the left side, about 0.8 miles from the stop sign {1}. The trailhead is across the road from the west end of the parking area. There are toilets at the parking area.

Description: Fay Canyon is one of our favorite hikes for non-hiker guests because it is short (only about 2.2 miles round trip), relatively level, and very scenic. The trail essentially ends at a massive rock slide {4}.

And for those wanting a greater challenge, there is a side trail located about 0.5 mile from the main parking area that leads to a natural stone arch {2}. You'll have to scramble up about 225 feet on this unmarked trail if you want to see the arch, which is located up next to the cliff face {3}. This will add about 0.5 mile to the hike. This side trail is narrow and steep with cactus along the edges and loose rock so watch your footing. There is a narrow slot up under the arch where the rocks have separated and you can "disappear" into the opening. Some people suggest that the area under the arch is a powerful vortex spot. (Additional information on vortexes can be found on page 6.)

More Photos: Scan the QR code for more photos of this trail

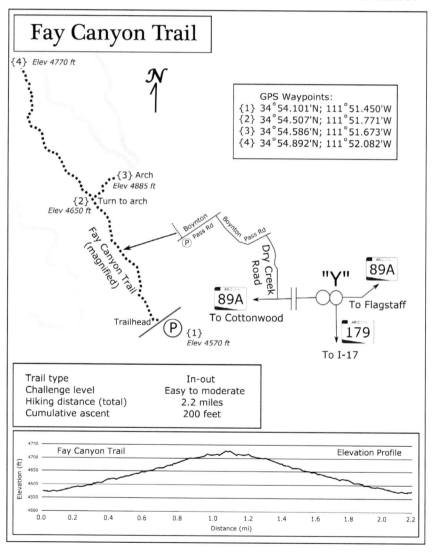

Fay Canyon Trail

{4} Elev 4770 ft

N

GPS Waypoints:
{1} 34°54.101'N; 111°51.450'W
{2} 34°54.507'N; 111°51.771'W
{3} 34°54.586'N; 111°51.673'W
{4} 34°54.892'N; 111°52.082'W

{3} Arch
Elev 4885 ft

{2} Turn to arch
Elev 4650 ft

Fay Canyon Trail (magnified)

Boynton Pass Rd

Boynton Pass Rd

P

Dry Creek Road

"Y"

89A

89A
To Cottonwood

To Flagstaff

179

To I-17

Trailhead

P {1}
Elev 4570 ft

Trail type	In-out
Challenge level	Easy to moderate
Hiking distance (total)	2.2 miles
Cumulative ascent	200 feet

Fay Canyon Trail   Elevation Profile

Elevation (ft)

4750
4700
4650
4600
4550
4500

0.0   0.2   0.4   0.6   0.8   1.0   1.2   1.4   1.6   1.8   2.0   2.2
Distance (mi)

HS Canyon Trail

Summary: A pleasant in-out hike through a narrow, forested canyon

Challenge Level: Moderate

Hiking Distance: About 2.1 miles each way or 4.2 miles round trip

Hiking Time: About 2 ½ hours round trip

Trail Popularity:

Trailhead Directions: From the "Y" roundabout (see page 5), drive west toward Cottonwood on SR 89A about 3 miles. Turn right on Dry Creek Road (where speed limits are strictly enforced). Stay on Dry Creek Road for 2 miles then turn right on Forest Road (FR) 152. Proceed on FR 152 for 3.4 miles to the Secret Canyon parking area on your left {1}.

Note: FR 152 is an extremely rough road beyond the 0.2 mile paved section; a high clearance vehicle is necessary and 4WD is recommended.

Description: To reach the HS Trail, you begin hiking the Secret Canyon Trail. You'll cross a wash after 0.6 mile {2}. Look to the right because after a rain there is a nice small pool of water. Proceed another 0.1 mile and you'll see the HS Canyon Trail #50 sign on your left {3}. The HS Canyon Trail gently rises about 625 feet providing good red rock views, although the forest of alligator junipers, oak and pinion pines obscures some of them. You'll find a lot of manzanita along the trail. At higher elevations on the trail, more manzanita trees appear among the manzanita bushes. You'll come to a nice spot for a photo after 1 mile {4}. As

44

you proceed, the trail becomes somewhat overgrown – a result of its relative inaccessibility because of the poor condition of FR 152.

The name (HS Trail) reportedly comes from the early riders finding lots of horse s**t on this trail. When the Forest Service officially named the trail, they kept the initials (HS) but named it after Henry Schuerman, an early Sedona resident. The HS Canyon Trail is a good hike in the summer as there is plenty of shade. The trail ends next to Maroon Mountain {5}.

More Photos: Scan the QR code for more photos of this trail

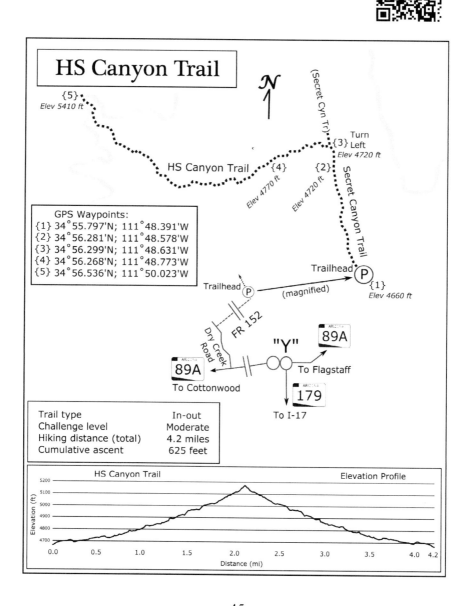

Huckaby Trail

as a two-vehicle hike

Summary: An in-out or two-vehicle hike descending from Schnebly Hill Road to the banks of Oak Creek with a great view of Midgley Bridge

Challenge Level: Moderate

Hiking Distance: About 2.5 miles each way or 5 miles round trip; or 3 miles

Hiking Time: About 3 hours round trip as an in-out hike; about 2 hours as a two vehicle hike

Trail Popularity: 🚶🚶

Trailhead Directions: From the "Y" roundabout (see page 5), drive south on SR 179 about 0.3 mile to the Schnebly Hill roundabout then drive 270 degrees (3/4 of the way) around to Schnebly Hill Road. Proceed on the paved Schnebly Hill Road for 1 mile then turn left into the parking area {1}. The trailhead parking is shared with the Munds Wagon Trail. The trail begins on the west side of the parking area. There are toilets at the parking area. If you are doing a two-vehicle hike, park the other vehicle at the Midgley Bridge parking area (see Wilson Canyon Trail directions).

Description: The Huckaby Trail begins in a westerly direction from the parking area. You'll soon intersect the Marg's Draw Trail on the left. Huckaby then turns north and crosses Bear Wallow Wash. The trail rises and falls as you approach Oak Creek Canyon. After about 0.7 mile look for an overlook on the left {2} for a nice view of Uptown Sedona and Wilson Mountain. After about 1.6 miles you'll have your first view of Midgley Bridge {3}. Look around for the views of "Lucy," "Snoopy," Cathedral Rock and many other named rock formations.

As you approach Oak Creek, the trail descends quite steeply {4}. At the 2 mile mark you'll be down in the flood plain along Oak Creek and there is shade provided by the riparian trees. Watch for poison ivy along the trail. Unless the water is low and you want to cross to the other side of Oak Creek by doing some rock-hopping {6}, end the hike where you have an awesome view of Midgley Bridge, just north of Uptown Sedona {5}. If you continue across Oak Creek, you'll hike up about 150 feet and turn west to reach Midgley Bridge. You can make this hike a two-vehicle hike – one vehicle parked at the Schnebly Hill

Road parking area {1} and the other parked at Midgley Bridge {7}. Just make sure you can cross Oak Creek.

Note: There is no shade for the first 2 miles of this hike so it is a hot summer hike.

More Photos: Scan the QR code for more photos of this trail

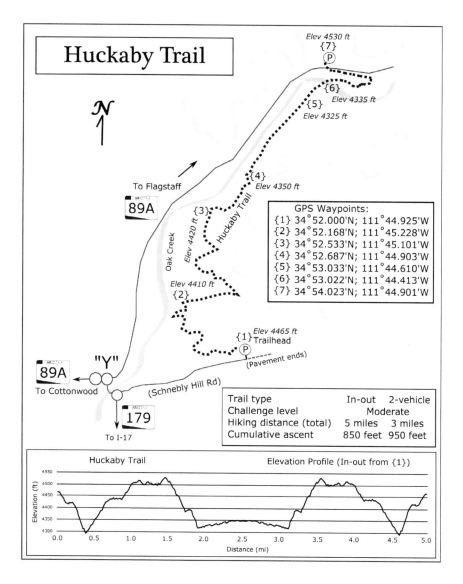

GPS Waypoints:
{1} 34°52.000'N; 111°44.925'W
{2} 34°52.168'N; 111°45.228'W
{3} 34°52.533'N; 111°45.101'W
{4} 34°52.687'N; 111°44.903'W
{5} 34°53.033'N; 111°44.610'W
{6} 34°53.022'N; 111°44.413'W
{7} 34°54.023'N; 111°44.901'W

Trail type	In-out	2-vehicle
Challenge level	Moderate	
Hiking distance (total)	5 miles	3 miles
Cumulative ascent	850 feet	950 feet

47

Jim Thompson Trail

Summary: An in-out hike around the south edge of Steamboat Rock overlooking Midgley Bridge

Challenge Level: Moderate

Hiking Distance: About 2.7 miles each way or 5.4 miles round trip

Hiking Time: About 3 hours round trip

Trail Popularity: 🚶🚶

Trailhead Directions: From the "Y" roundabout (see page 5), drive north on SR 89A about 0.3 mile to Jordan Road. Turn left on Jordan Road then drive to the end. Turn left on West Park Ridge Drive then proceed through the paved cul-de-sac, continuing on the dirt road for 0.5 mile to the parking area {1}. There are toilets at the parking area.

Description: Built by Jim Thompson in the 1880s as a road to a homestead at Indian Gardens, the trail begins on the northeast side of the parking area {2}. You'll begin by hiking north then quickly turn right and begin hiking south. After hiking 0.4 mile, you'll intersect the end of the Jordan Trail {3}. In another 0.3 mile you'll come to an old gate frame. You'll be hiking in an easterly direction along Jim Thompson's old wagon road toward the base of Steamboat Rock.

There isn't much shade on this hike so it will be hot in the summer. There are excellent views to the north. The views to the south include Cathedral Rock and

Uptown Sedona. Because you are looking into the sun, photographs to the south can be a challenge.

We usually stop after about 2.5 miles where you can see Midgley Bridge and look across Oak Creek Canyon {4}. If you continue on for about 0.25 mile, you'll intersect the Wilson Canyon Trail {5} after descending about 125 feet.

More Photos: Scan the QR code for more photos of this trail

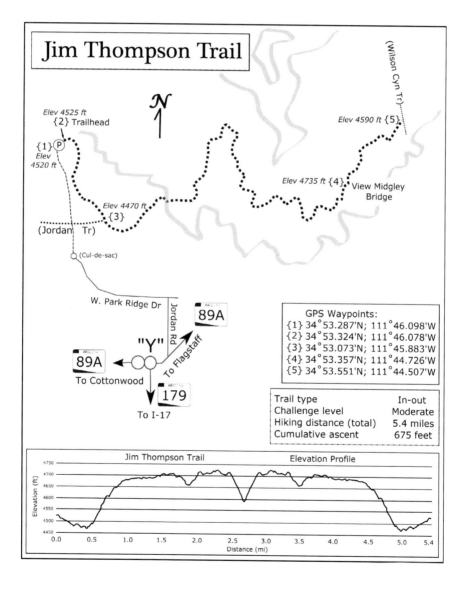

Jordan Trail

Summary: An in-out partially shaded hike near town that ends at the Soldier Pass Trail

Challenge Level: Easy to Moderate

Hiking Distance: About 1.6 miles each way or 3.2 miles round trip

Hiking Time: About 2 hours round trip

Trail Popularity: 🚶🚶 🚶🚶 🚶🚶

Trailhead Directions: From the "Y" roundabout (see page 5), drive north on SR 89A about 0.3 mile to Jordan Road. Turn left on Jordan Road then drive to the end. Turn left on West Park Ridge Drive then proceed through the paved cul-de-sac, continuing on the dirt road for 0.5 mile to the parking area. There are toilets at the parking area. There are two trailheads for this trail. The trailhead at the parking area is on the west side, to the right of the toilets. If you walk back down the road 0.4 mile there is another Jordan Trail signpost {2}.

Description: If you begin the hike from the parking area, you'll hike a short distance to the west, then turn south. After 0.4 mile, you'll intersect the second Jordan Trail {3}. Turn right (west) then begin hiking the main trail somewhat uphill as you hike along an old road. If you turn left (east), you'll cross the road then intersect the Jim Thompson Trail after 0.2 mile.

The views gradually improve as you continue the hike. You'll intersect the Javelina Trail after another 0.3 mile {4}, come to the Ant Hill Trail then intersect the Cibola Trail at the 1.4 mile mark {5}. Continue on the Jordan Trail until you intersect the Soldier Pass Trail at Devil's Kitchen, which is the largest sinkhole in the Sedona area {6}.

If you want to continue a little further, hike north on the Soldier Pass Trail for 0.4 mile to the Seven Sacred Pools {7}. You can retrace your route or hike back on the Cibola Trail to the parking area. The Jordan Trail is popular with mountain bicyclists so you may encounter them on the trail.

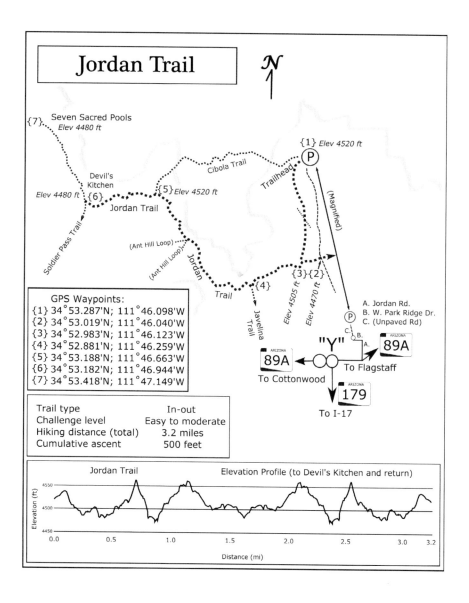

Jordan Trail

N

{7} Seven Sacred Pools
Elev 4480 ft

{1} *Elev 4520 ft*
℗

Cibola Trail

Devil's Kitchen
Elev 4480 ft {6}
{5} *Elev 4520 ft*
Jordan Trail
Trailhead

(Magnified)

Soldier Pass Trail

(Ant Hill Loop)
(Ant Hill Loop)
Jordan

{3} {2}
Elev 4505 ft
Elev 4470 ft

Trail
{4}

Javelina Trail

℗

A. Jordan Rd.
B. W. Park Ridge Dr.
C. (Unpaved Rd)

C.
B.
A.

"Y"

ARIZONA
89A

ARIZONA
89A

To Flagstaff

To Cottonwood

ARIZONA
179

To I-17

GPS Waypoints:
{1} 34°53.287'N; 111°46.098'W
{2} 34°53.019'N; 111°46.040'W
{3} 34°52.983'N; 111°46.123'W
{4} 34°52.881'N; 111°46.259'W
{5} 34°53.188'N; 111°46.663'W
{6} 34°53.182'N; 111°46.944'W
{7} 34°53.418'N; 111°47.149'W

Trail type	In-out
Challenge level	Easy to moderate
Hiking distance (total)	3.2 miles
Cumulative ascent	500 feet

Jordan Trail   Elevation Profile (to Devil's Kitchen and return)

Elevation (ft)

4550

4500

4450

0.0   0.5   1.0   1.5   2.0   2.5   3.0   3.2

Distance (mi)

Little Horse Trail ★

Summary: A lovely in-out hike to Chicken Point, a large slickrock knoll with majestic views

Challenge Level: Moderate

Hiking Distance: About 2 miles each way or 4 miles round trip

Hiking Time: About 2 hours round trip

Trail Popularity: 🚶🚶🚶🚶

Trailhead Directions: From the "Y" roundabout (see page 5), drive south on SR 179 about 3.5 miles. You'll see a "Scenic View" and a hiking sign on the right side of SR 179 just past the Back O' Beyond roundabout. Turn left here then proceed across the median to the parking area {1}. There are toilets at the parking area.

Description: You'll begin by hiking south on the Bell Rock Pathway for 0.3 mile until it intersects the beginning of the Little Horse Trail {2}. Turn left here to begin the Little Horse Trail. When you come to a dry wash, turn left to cross the wash then follow the trail east then north toward the Twin Buttes, an impressive red rock formation. After about 1 mile, you'll intersect the Llama Trail on the right {3}. You will intersect the Chapel Trail at the 1.4 mile mark {4}. If you have the time, follow the Chapel Trail for 0.5 mile until it intersects Chapel Road to go up to visit the Chapel of the Holy Cross {5}. Returning to the Little Horse Trail, continue on for another 0.4 mile and you'll arrive at an expansive area of slickrock known as Chicken Point. The climb up to Chicken

Point isn't hard and is well worth the effort {6}. Chicken Point is named for thrill-seeking jeep drivers who once dared to drive close to the edge of the point (jeep access is no longer permitted on Chicken Point). If you look to the south, you'll see a "chicken-shaped" rock high up on the red rock cliff. Chicken Point is a nice place for a snack break as the views are outstanding. You'll likely encounter some Pink Jeeps as the "Broken Arrow" tour brings many visitors to this beautiful area.

More Photos: Scan the QR code for more photos of this trail

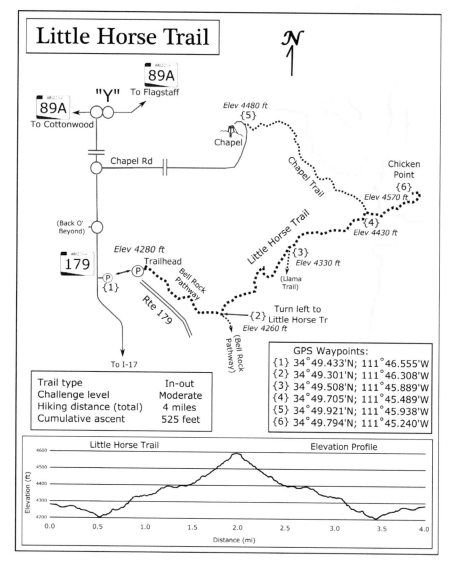

Llama Trail

Summary: A loop hike with panoramic views of many of Sedona's famous rock formations

Challenge Level: Easy to Moderate

Hiking Distance: About 4.4 miles for the Llama/Bail/Bell Rock Pathway loop; about 6 miles for the Llama/Little Horse/ Bell Rock Pathway/Phone Trail loop

Hiking Time: About 3 hours round trip for the Llama/Little Horse/Bell Rock Pathway/Phone Trail Loop

Trail Popularity: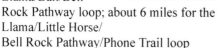

Trailhead Directions: From the "Y" roundabout (see page 5), drive south on SR 179 for about 5 miles to the parking area. After you drive about 3.2 miles, just past the Back O' Beyond roundabout, SR 179 becomes a divided highway. Continue driving south. About 1.8 miles beyond the Back O' Beyond roundabout, southbound SR 179 adds a passing lane on the left. From the passing lane, turn left at the sign for the "Court House Vista" parking area {1} (it's the second scenic view on the left side of SR 179). Before you turn, you'll see Bell Rock ahead of you on the left side of SR 179. There are toilets at the parking area. The trail starts on the southeast side of the parking area. There is another Llama trailhead off of the Little Horse Trail {8}.

Description: The Llama Trail goes from Bell Rock to the Little Horse Trail. It is a favorite of mountain bicyclists. We prefer to hike it as a loop hike. From the parking area, proceed past the interpretive signboard and follow the Bell Rock Trail 0.1 mile to the intersection with the Bell Rock Pathway {2}. Turn left (northeast) and follow the Bell Rock Pathway 0.3 mile. Continue straight ahead on to the Courthouse Butte Loop Trail {3}. Follow Courthouse Butte Loop for about 300 feet then turn left onto the Llama Trail {4}.

In 0.9 mile you'll come to a scenic area with 8 depressions in the slickrock that are usually filled with water {5}. Continue another 0.8 mile to the intersection with the Bail Trail {6}. You can turn left here and follow the Bail Trail 0.4 mile to the intersection with the Bell Rock Pathway {7}, or continue 1 mile on the

Llama Trail to the Little Horse Trail {8} then turn left to reach the Bell Rock Pathway {9}. Hike south on the Bell Rock Pathway then turn on to the Phone Trail {10} for a shortcut back to the parking area. The Llama Trail approaches Lee Mountain and provides outstanding views of Bell Rock, Courthouse Butte, Twin Buttes and Cathedral Rock. There isn't much shade on this hike so it would be a good choice in cooler weather.

More Photos: Scan the QR code for more photos of this trail

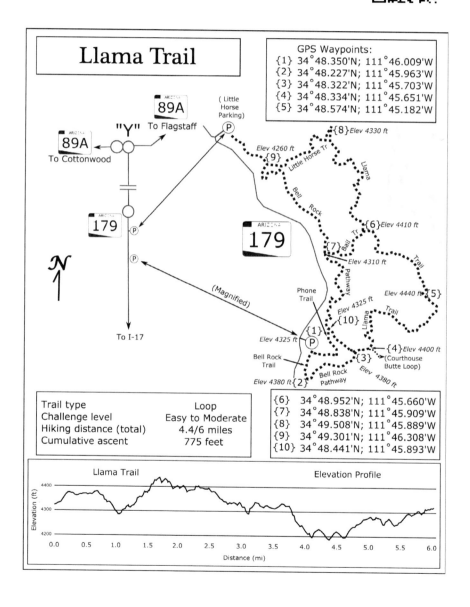

Trail type	Loop
Challenge level	Easy to Moderate
Hiking distance (total)	4.4/6 miles
Cumulative ascent	775 feet

Lost Canyon Trail

Summary: An in-out hike to an overlook of some Indian ruins

Challenge Level: Moderate

Hiking Distance: About 1 mile each way or 2 miles round trip

Hiking Time: About 1 ½ hours round trip

Trail Popularity: 🚶

Trailhead Directions: From the "Y" roundabout (see page 5), drive west toward Cottonwood on SR 89A about 3 miles. Turn right on Dry Creek Road (where speed limits are strictly enforced). Stay on Dry Creek Road for 2 miles then turn right on Forest Road (FR) 152. Proceed on FR 152 for 2.5 miles to the parking area on your right {1}. The parking area is for the west end of the Brins Mesa Trail.

Note: FR 152 is an extremely rough road beyond the 0.2 mile paved section; a high clearance vehicle is necessary and 4WD is recommended.

Description: This is an unmarked, unmaintained trail that includes a sharp climb to view some undisturbed Indian ruins below. Hike the Brins Mesa Trail for some 225 feet (about 75 paces) then turn right to the unmarked Lost Canyon Trail {2}. The red rock views along the trail are very nice. You'll need to watch for improvised cairns to find the trail in places. The trail gradually rises for the first 0.3 mile {3} then you begin a steep climb of 275 feet to reach the top of a mesa {4}. As you hike across the mesa for 0.2 mile, the trail comes close to the mesa edge {5}. Continue along the edge of the mesa. There are some impressive red rocks that have fallen from the cliff on your left. To see the ruins below the edge of the mesa, you have to approach the edge of a sheer drop-off; the view is spectacular, but use extreme caution {6}.

We recommend using a portable GPS unit to hike this trail (go to http://greatsedonahikes.com/gps/gps.html).

More Photos: Scan the QR code for more photos of this trail

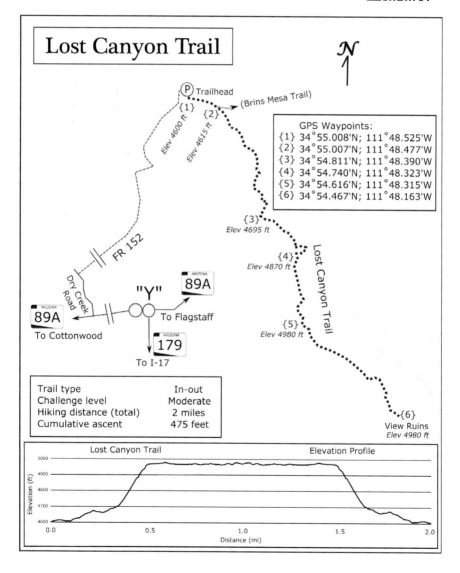

Mescal Trail

Summary: An in-out hike that skirts the base of Mescal Mountain with both panoramic and up close red rock views with the option for a loop hike

Challenge Level: Easy to Moderate.

Hiking Distance: About 2.4 miles each way to the Deadman's Pass Trail intersection or 4.8 miles round trip; about 5 miles for Mescal Trail to Deadman's Pass Trail to Long Canyon Trail loop

Hiking Time: About 2 ½ hours for the in-out hike to Deadman's Pass Trail round trip; about 3 hours for the Long Canyon loop round trip

Trail Popularity: 🚶🚶🚶

Trailhead Directions: From the "Y" roundabout (see page 5), drive west toward Cottonwood on SR 89A about 3 miles. Turn right on Dry Creek Road (where speed limits are strictly enforced). Stay on Dry Creek Road to a stop sign (about 3 miles) then turn right on Long Canyon Road. Proceed 0.3 mile to the parking area on the right and park at the northeast (far) end {1}. The trail begins across the road from the northeast end of the parking area.

Description: This is a nice trail that provides both close-up and distant red rock views. After the first 0.1 mile, the trail begins to gently rise as you approach the base of Mescal Mountain. At 0.25 mile, you'll intersect the connector trail to Long Canyon Trail on your right {2}. Continue straight ahead. At 0.4 mile, you are on the top of a high bluff with good red rock views all around. You'll pass a cairn and trail marker for the Yucca Trail {3} then at the 1 mile mark, look up high to the right you'll observe a large cave in the side of Mescal Mountain {4}. Soon the trail becomes very narrow in places and there are steep drop offs – watch your footing. Don't attempt this trail if it is snowy or the trail is icy. You'll find signs indicating "Difficult" and "Extreme" for the mountain bikers. We recommend you hike the "Difficult" path. After 1.75 miles, you'll come to a cairn and trail marker for the Canyon of Fools Trail [5]. Just beyond you can see Kachina Woman in Boynton Canyon, Cockscomb, Doe Mountain, Bear Mountain and Courthouse Butte in the distance.

As you proceed, the views get better and better. At 2.2 miles [6], the trail begins to descend some 85 feet in 0.25 mile to intersect the Deadman's Pass Trail [7]. Although we prefer to return via the same route, if you wish to hike a loop, turn right on to the Deadman's Pass Trail and hike for 0.9 mile to the Long Canyon Trail. Turn right on to the Long Canyon Trail {8} then follow it back toward Long Canyon Road. You'll see a connector trail just before the parking area on Long Canyon Road {9}. Turn right to follow the connector trail back to the Mescal Trail. Turn left when you reach the intersection with the Mescal Trail {2} to return to the parking area {1}.

Note: There are some places where the trail is narrow with drop offs on the side.

More Photos: Scan the QR code for more photos of this trail

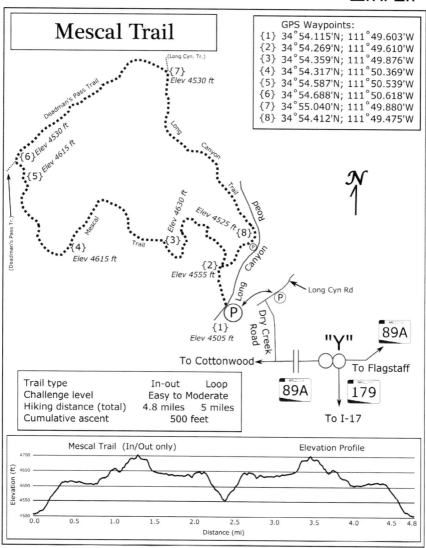

Trail type	In-out	Loop
Challenge level	Easy to Moderate	
Hiking distance (total)	4.8 miles	5 miles
Cumulative ascent	500 feet	

GPS Waypoints:
{1} 34°54.115'N; 111°49.603'W
{2} 34°54.269'N; 111°49.610'W
{3} 34°54.359'N; 111°49.876'W
{4} 34°54.317'N; 111°50.369'W
{5} 34°54.587'N; 111°50.539'W
{6} 34°54.688'N; 111°50.618'W
{7} 34°55.040'N; 111°49.880'W
{8} 34°54.412'N; 111°49.475'W

Pyramid Loop Trail

Summary: A loop hike circling the "great pyramid," which is visible from the end of the Tabletop Trail off the west side of the Airport Loop Trail

Challenge Level: Easy to Moderate

Hiking Distance: About 2.3 miles round trip

Hiking Time: About 2 hours round trip

Trail Popularity: 🚶🚶

Trailhead Directions: From the "Y" roundabout (see page 5), drive west on SR 89A about 4.25 miles then turn left on the Upper Red Rock Loop Road. Sedona High School is on your right. Follow the Upper Red Rock Loop Road for 1.8 miles to the intersection of Chavez Ranch Road then park on the right side of the road {1}. There is room for about 12 vehicles here. You'll see the trail to the west from the parking area.

Description: This former mountain bike trail was opened in February 2016. In earlier editions of Great Sedona Hikes, we had a trail we called the Pyramid Trail which is now part of the Scorpion Trail. This new Pyramid Trail (combined with the Scorpion Trail) circles around the base of the Pyramid rock formation. You'll need good hiking boots with excellent traction because there are places where the trail is steep with loose gravel.

To hike the loop, you'll hike part of the Scorpion and the Pyramid Trails. From the parking area, hike west for 300 feet to the signpost at the intersection of the Scorpion and Pyramid Trails {2}. You'll come back here on the return trip. We suggest you hike the loop in the counterclockwise direction for the best views. So turn right and follow the Scorpion Trail. This trail gently rises for the next mile. You'll pass by a fence after 0.5 mile {3} and have a nice view behind you after 0.8 mile {4}. After 1 mile, you'll intersect the Pyramid Trail on your left at the signpost and large cairn {5}. Make a very sharp left turn here to follow the Pyramid Trail.

The Pyramid Trail is relatively flat for about the next 0.4 mile. You'll come to another nice view of Cathedral Rock {6} and begin a rather steep descent. There are excellent views all along this section of the trail. But the trail here is very narrow, with loose dirt and rocks as well as uneven in places with large drop offs so watch your footing. There's a nice place to stop for a snack just before you make a sharp right turn at about the 1.6 mile mark {7}. You'll have continuing views of Cathedral Rock on your way back to the intersection of the Pyramid and Scorpion Trails {2}. When you arrive back, continue straight ahead to return to the parking area {1}.

Note: There is little shade on this hike so it is good choice for cooler weather.

More Photos: Scan the QR code for more photos of this trail

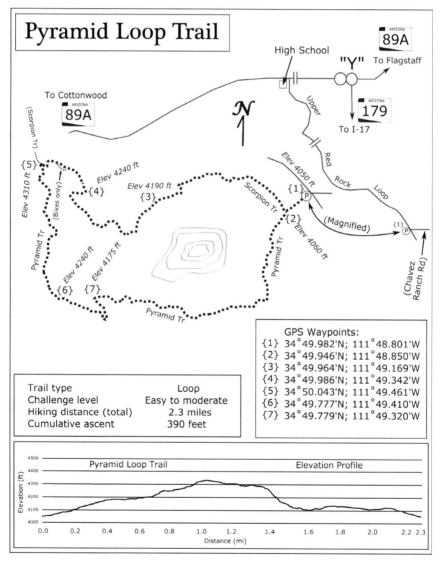

Soldier Pass Trail ★

Summary: An in-out hike with stops at the Devil's Kitchen and the Seven Sacred Pools along with a side trip to some impressive red rock arches

Challenge Level: Moderate

Hiking Distance: About 2.1 miles one way to the Brins Mesa Trail or 4.2 miles round trip

Hiking Time: About 3 hours round trip

Trail Popularity:

Trailhead Directions: From the "Y" roundabout (see page 5), drive west toward Cottonwood on SR 89A for 1.25 miles then turn right on Soldiers Pass Road. Proceed on Soldiers Pass for 1.5 miles. Turn right on Rim Shadows. Go approximately 0.25 mile then turn left into the parking area {1}. The gate to the parking area is open from 8:00 am to 6:00 pm. If you get back to your car after 6:00 pm, you won't be able to drive out of the parking area. There is room for only about 12 vehicles here so try to come early or you may have to wait for a parking spot. There is no parking on adjacent streets.

Description: Shortly after beginning the Soldier Pass Trail, you'll descend into the deep Soldier Wash then climb up to the Devil's Kitchen (about 0.2 mile) {2}. This is the largest sinkhole in the Sedona area. After another 0.4 mile, you'll come to the Seven Sacred Pools, which are small depressions in the red rock that hold water even in dry periods {3}. These two areas are very popular with visitors on jeep rides and hikers. You won't encounter jeeps or as many other hikers on the rest of the trail. There is partial shade beginning at about the 1 mile mark and the trees tend to block some of the red rock views.

About 1.3 miles from the trailhead, look to the right for a faint trail up to the Soldier Pass Arches {4}. It's a steep climb of about 275 feet but being beneath the arches is very nice. Return to the main trail. As you continue, the trail becomes rockier and steeper as it climbs up to Brins Mesa. Once on top of Brins Mesa, you'll come to a fork at the 2 mile mark {6}. Take the right fork to an overlook {8} or take the left fork to the intersection with the Brins Mesa Trail after another 0.1 mile {7}.

Turn around here, or you can turn right on to the Brins Mesa Trail then follow it for about 2.2 miles to the parking area off of Jordan Road. From there you can hike the Cibola and Jordan Trails west for about 1 mile to the Soldier Pass Trail. Here, you'd turn left and follow Soldiers Pass Trail back to the parking area making a loop hike of about 5.8 miles.

More Photos: Scan the QR code for more photos of this trail

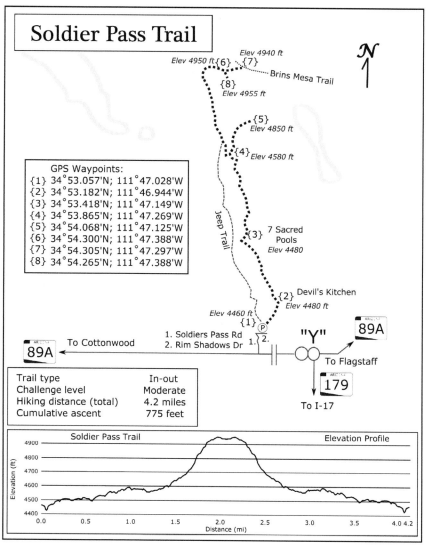

Soldier Pass Trail

GPS Waypoints:	
{1} 34°53.057'N; 111°47.028'W	
{2} 34°53.182'N; 111°46.944'W	
{3} 34°53.418'N; 111°47.149'W	
{4} 34°53.865'N; 111°47.269'W	
{5} 34°54.068'N; 111°47.125'W	
{6} 34°54.300'N; 111°47.388'W	
{7} 34°54.305'N; 111°47.297'W	
{8} 34°54.265'N; 111°47.388'W	

Elev 4940 ft
Elev 4950 ft {6} {7}
Brins Mesa Trail
{8}
Elev 4955 ft

{5}
Elev 4850 ft

{4} Elev 4580 ft

Jeep Trail

{3} 7 Sacred Pools
Elev 4480

{2} Devil's Kitchen
Elev 4480 ft

Elev 4460 ft
{1}

1. Soldiers Pass Rd
2. Rim Shadows Dr

To Cottonwood

89A

"Y"

89A

To Flagstaff

179

To I-17

Trail type	In-out
Challenge level	Moderate
Hiking distance (total)	4.2 miles
Cumulative ascent	775 feet

Soldier Pass Trail   Elevation Profile

Elevation (ft)
4900
4800
4700
4600
4500
4400
0.0   0.5   1.0   1.5   2.0   2.5   3.0   3.5   4.0 4.2
Distance (mi)

Sterling Pass to Vultee Arch Trails

Summary: An in-out or a two-vehicle "pass-the-key" hike up the west side of Oak Creek Canyon then down to Secret Mountain Wilderness

Challenge Level: Hard

Hiking Distance: About 4.5 miles from the Sterling Pass parking area to the Vultee Arch parking area as a "pass-the-key" hike; about 2.6 miles each way from Sterling Pass trailhead to Vultee Arch or 5.2 miles round trip

Hiking Time: About 2 ½ hours as a "pass-the-key" hike round trip; about 3 ½ hours to Vultee Arch and return round trip

Trail Popularity: 🚶

Trailhead Directions: From the "Y" roundabout (see page 5), drive north on SR 89A about 6.25 miles. You'll need to find a wide spot in the road to park on the west side near mile marker 360.4, about 300 feet north of the Manzanita campground. The trail starts on the west side of SR 89A {1}.

We prefer to do this hike as a "pass-the-key" two-vehicle hike (i.e. two groups hiking toward each other from the two separate trailheads and exchanging their vehicle keys) with one vehicle parked at the Sterling Pass trailhead and the other parked at the Vultee Arch trailhead at the end of FR 152 {4} (see the Vultee Arch Trail for trailhead directions).

Description: The trail is steep. There are still many fallen trees from the Brins Fire in 2006. You'll hike up about 1150 feet to reach the saddle {2} then enter a pine forest. The saddle is about 1.4 miles from the SR 89A parking area. As you continue from the saddle, the trail begins a steady descent.

About 2.4 miles in, you'll come to the sign for Vultee Arch on the right {3}. Hike 0.2 mile down the Vultee Arch Trail to see Vultee Arch, an impressive sight (see Vultee Arch Trail hike description) {5}. If you only have one vehicle, retrace your steps back to your vehicle parked along SR 89A.

More Photos: Scan the QR code for more photos of this trail

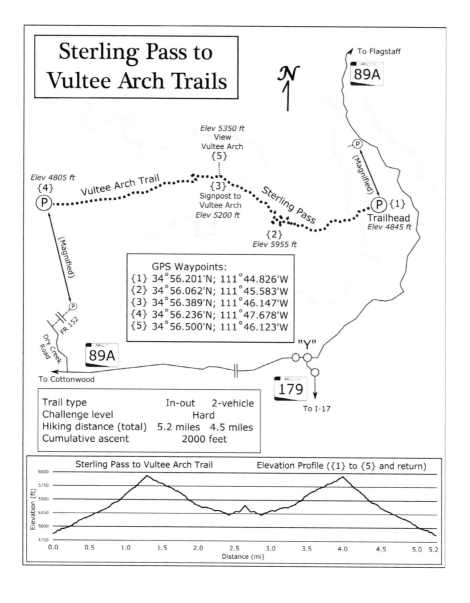

Templeton Trail

Summary: A two-vehicle "pass-the-key" or in-out hike with views of Sedona's major rock formations

Challenge Level: Moderate

Hiking Distance: About 4.6 miles from the Court House Vista parking area to the Baldwin Loop Trail parking area; about 9.2 miles in-out

Hiking Time: About 2 ½ hours as a "pass-the-key" hike; about 5 hours as an in-out hike from the Court House Vista parking area to the Baldwin Loop Trail parking area and return

Trail Popularity: 🚶🚶🚶

Trailhead Directions: Park one vehicle at the Court House Vista parking area {1} (see Bell Rock Loop and Bell Rock Vortex parking directions on page 26) and one vehicle at the Baldwin Loop Trail parking area {7} (see Baldwin Loop Trail parking directions on page 20).

Description: The Templeton Trail extends northwest from Bell Rock Pathway, just north of Bell Rock and Courthouse Butte to the Baldwin Loop Trail near Oak Creek and Red Rock Crossing. It provides excellent views of Bell Rock, Courthouse Butte, Lee Mountain, Cathedral Rock and many other red rock formations. There are several ways to hike this trail. You can do this hike as a "pass-the-key" two-vehicle hike (i.e. two groups hiking toward each other from the two separate trailheads and exchanging their vehicle keys). If you hike from the Court House Vista parking area, look for the Phone Trail on your left about 200 feet past the interpretive signboard {2}. Follow the Phone Trail 0.3 mile then continue north on the Bell Rock Pathway Trail. In 0.1 mile turn left on to the Templeton Trail {3} then follow it beneath both the northbound and southbound lanes of SR 179. You'll have excellent views of Cathedral Rock ahead and, in 1 mile, you'll intersect the HT Trail on your right {4}. As you approach Cathedral Rock, the landscape becomes high desert.

You'll intersect the Cathedral Rock Trail in another 1.3 miles on your right {5} and the short but steep trail to the "saddle" of Cathedral Rock in another 200 feet on your left. As you continue on the Templeton Trail, you'll descend a series of switchbacks. In 0.8 mile, you'll be adjacent to Oak Creek, across from "Buddha Beach" and Red Rock Crossing. The Templeton Trail continues on for another 0.2 mile where it ends at the Baldwin Loop Trail {6}. Continue straight ahead on the Baldwin Loop Trail for another 0.5 mile to the Baldwin Loop Trail parking area on Verde Valley School Road {7} for a hike of 4.6 miles.

More Photos: Scan the QR code for more photos of this trail

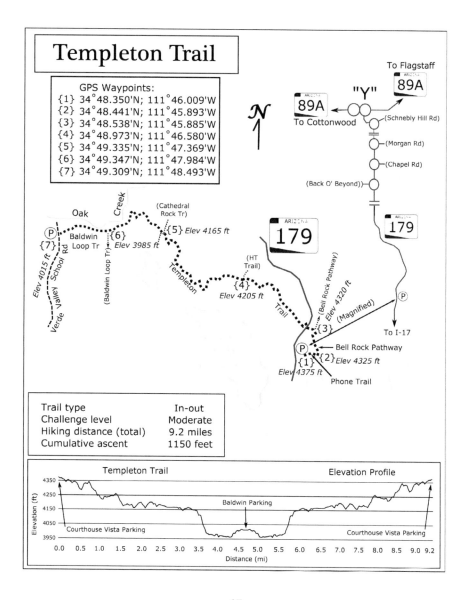

Templeton Trail

GPS Waypoints:
{1} 34°48.350'N; 111°46.009'W
{2} 34°48.441'N; 111°45.893'W
{3} 34°48.538'N; 111°45.885'W
{4} 34°48.973'N; 111°46.580'W
{5} 34°49.335'N; 111°47.369'W
{6} 34°49.347'N; 111°47.984'W
{7} 34°49.309'N; 111°48.493'W

To Flagstaff

89A

"Y"

89A
To Cottonwood

(Schnebly Hill Rd)
(Morgan Rd)
(Chapel Rd)
(Back O' Beyond)

179

179

Oak Creek

(Cathedral Rock Tr)
{5} Elev 4165 ft

Baldwin {6}
{7} Loop Tr Elev 3985 ft

Elev 4015 ft
Verde Valley School Rd
(Baldwin Loop Tr)

Templeton Trail

(HT Trail)
{4}
Elev 4205 ft

(Bell Rock Pathway)
Elev 4320 ft
(Magnified)

P
To I-17

{3}

P Bell Rock Pathway
{1} {2} Elev 4325 ft
Elev 4375 ft
Phone Trail

Trail type	In-out
Challenge level	Moderate
Hiking distance (total)	9.2 miles
Cumulative ascent	1150 feet

Templeton Trail   Elevation Profile

4350
4250
4150
4050
3950
Elevation (ft)

Baldwin Parking

Courthouse Vista Parking

Courthouse Vista Parking

0.0 0.5 1.0 1.5 2.0 2.5 3.0 3.5 4.0 4.5 5.0 5.5 6.0 6.5 7.0 7.5 8.0 8.5 9.0 9.2
Distance (mi)

West Fork Trail ★

Summary:
A beautiful, shady in-out hike along a flowing creek

Challenge Level:
Moderate

Hiking Distance:
About 3.6 miles each way or 7.2 miles round trip

Hiking Time: About 3 ½ hours round trip

Trail Popularity: 🚶🚶🚶🚶

Trailhead Directions: From the "Y" roundabout (see page 5), drive north on SR 89A about 10.5 miles. Turn left into the parking area {1}. The trail starts on the far side of the parking area, furthest away from the entrance. There are toilets at the parking area. The gate to the parking area opens at 8:00 am: use a prepay envelope if the parking attendant isn't on duty. The parking area fills quickly so be there early in the morning. Be sure to check on the current closing time so that your vehicle isn't trapped by the locked gates when you return.

Description: West Fork is considered by many to be the most beautiful trail in the Sedona area. It is a special fee area (see Required Parking Pass, page 7). You'll be crossing the water 13 times as you hike the trail. You have to step from stone to stone to cross, so the hike isn't recommended in high water times (you'll get your feet wet!!). After 0.3 mile you'll come to the remains of Mayhew's Lodge, built in the 1880s. It was remodeled in 1895 then burned down in 1980 {2}.

At the 0.4 mile, mark you'll come to the first of the 13 creek crossings {3}. As you continue along, look to the sides for some amazing red rock bluffs. There is a nice spot to stop after 1 mile {4}. Just across the 10th creek crossing is a natural stone "bench" which is another nice place to stop and rest. At 2.2 miles, you'll come to a huge overhang where the water has eroded the rock {5}. Continue another 0.2 mile and watch for a short side trail to a cave on your left {6}. At 3.6 miles, you'll effectively come to the end of the trail because you'll have to wade through the water to continue {7}.

West Fork has two wonderful seasons, spring and fall. The most beautiful is fall, when the deciduous trees display glorious colors. The third week in October seems to be when the colors are usually at their peak.

More Photos: Scan the QR code for more photos of this trail

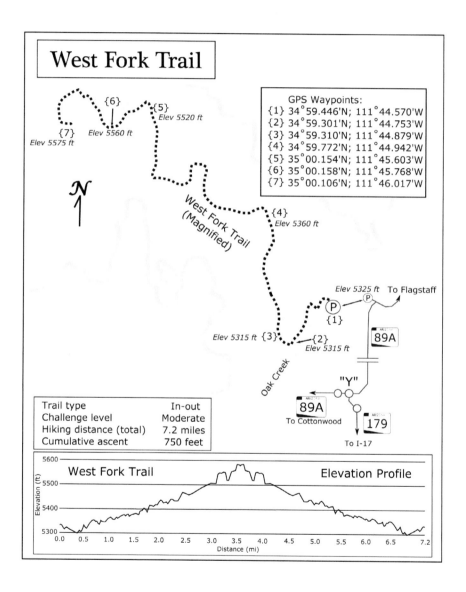

West Fork Trail

{6}

{5}
Elev 5520 ft

{7}
Elev 5575 ft

Elev 5560 ft

N

West Fork Trail
(Magnified)

{4}
Elev 5360 ft

Elev 5325 ft To Flagstaff

P
{1}

Elev 5315 ft {3}

{2}
Elev 5315 ft

89A

Oak Creek

"Y"

89A
To Cottonwood

179

To I-17

GPS Waypoints:	
{1}	34°59.446'N; 111°44.570'W
{2}	34°59.301'N; 111°44.753'W
{3}	34°59.310'N; 111°44.879'W
{4}	34°59.772'N; 111°44.942'W
{5}	35°00.154'N; 111°45.603'W
{6}	35°00.158'N; 111°45.768'W
{7}	35°00.106'N; 111°46.017'W

Trail type	In-out
Challenge level	Moderate
Hiking distance (total)	7.2 miles
Cumulative ascent	750 feet

West Fork Trail — Elevation Profile

Elevation (ft): 5600, 5500, 5400, 5300

Distance (mi): 0.0 0.5 1.0 1.5 2.0 2.5 3.0 3.5 4.0 4.5 5.0 5.5 6.0 6.5 7.2

Index

Made in the USA
San Bernardino, CA
23 September 2016